MARRIAGE
WRKS

A GUIDE TO A HAPPY LONG LASTING MARRIAGE

BY
JEANINE & MARK
EARNHART

Enjoy the work!

Jeanine Earnhart

Mark W. Earnhart

INTRODUCTION

Whether you are just starting out in a marriage or have been married many years, you already know that relationships have their ups and downs, no matter how hard you try. After being married for 40 years, we have probably been in your shoes at one time or another and hope that you will benefit by learning how we solved problems as they came up. Our book and our experiences are lovingly shared with you, in hopes that wherever you are in your relationship, you will gain something positive to add to your marriage. Obviously, it will be most beneficial to have both partners read the book.

At the end of each chapter, you will find a first hand experience from each of us, as well as a workbook page with questions to ask yourselves and write down your comments while they are fresh in your mind.

We encourage you to discuss your comments after each chapter with open hearts and minds, and no judgment towards each other's comments.

Table of Contents

MARRIAGE WORKS

Chains do not hold a marriage together.
It is threads, hundreds of tiny threads
which sew people together through the years.
Simone Signoret

We all have our ideas of what a good marriage should consist of, but many couples are having trouble reaching that goal in their relationship. One of the hurdles, as we see it, is that people are not very realistic about the expectations of marriage. Movies and books are filled with pixie-dusted scenarios of marriage. We have found the following to be a more accurate view of marriage:

No marriage is perfect all the time.
Happily ever after is best saved for the movies.
Marriages made in heaven have to live here on
 earth.
Wedded bliss comes in spurts.
When the bells stop ringing, the work begins.

The *good* news is that happy, healthy, loving, long-lasting marriages are possible.

7

Marriage is made up of two unique human beings going through their lives together, sharing the ups and downs of living, with love and caring as a base. There is no such thing as a perfect marriage. Anyone who tells you they have one, might be stretching the truth a little. A good marriage is forever changing, moving in different directions and constantly growing, but never quite "perfect".

The statistics vary, but the U.S. Bureau of Census gives us a figure of forty to fifty percent of marriages ending in divorce. There are certainly valid reasons for divorcing and we are aware that for many of the couples making up this number, divorce is the only answer. On the other hand, there are many couples divorcing because they have simply fallen out of love with each other and are not hearing bells anymore. If you are married long enough, you can expect that to happen now and then. The answer to these problems is not divorce; it is simply time to go to work on your marriage.

We've been frustrated over the years to see so many marriages end in divorce when the basic ingredients for a loving relationship were there all the time, but never used for lack of "know how." We've heard from newlyweds when the stars had left their eyes and we've shared with "Oldyweds" who were sick of living under the same roof year after year without having a meaningful conversation among other things.

The tools we have to share, apply to relationships that are brand new as well as those that have been around a long time and are just tired. Because each of us are individuals, with our own comfort zone, our ideas are not going to fit everyone's style. Our goal is to give couples a base to work from, adapt it comfortably to their relationship and grow along a customized path of their own.

In the 40 years we have been married, we have fallen in and out of "everlasting" love with each other many times. We've looked to different paths to find our way back. Some were successful and offered useful tools, while others didn't help us much at all. We found it ironic that authors who had many academic credentials, but had been through several divorces themselves, wrote many of the books written to help marriages. They knew what *not* to do, but at our troubled stage in marriage, we already knew what wasn't working. We needed advice on what *worked*. The best information we've been given over the years has been from couples that have been happily married for years. The academic letters following our names are not related to the subject of marriage, but have helped us to write this book in an interesting and creative way. In our

9

opinion, our most valuable knowledge to share with you comes with no degree, but from being happily married, (most of the time), for 40 years. The letters we offer as our credentials for this book are the MR. and MRS. in front of our names. We are not psychologists, marriage counselors or therapists. We have grown from teenagers to adulthood together, with struggles just like anyone else and have made it this far with a healthy, happy friendship that continues to grow. This book is not a biography of Jeanine & Mark Earnhart, although we will share a lot of our experiences with you in hopes of helping you to relate to an idea. Our goal is to share information and experiences that have been helpful to us and others in keeping a marriage healthy, alive, growing and loving. Although we have physically spent about 10 years writing this book, we have been working on it for 40 years. There have been days during our writing when our marriage was going over a bump in the road and we wondered, "What makes us think we qualify for giving advice to others when we aren't even *talking* to each other today?" Then, after talking out our problem and getting our marriage back on track we remembered, "Oh yeah. This is what we want to share with others."

We hope that whatever your stage in marriage, be it newlyweds, oldyweds or newlyweds *again,* you will be able to use this information to build a relationship that will last forever.

Contrary to popular belief, marriage *does* work. What many people don't realize is that marriage *is* work, so lets get to it.

Jeanine

Some people look at divorce as the "easy way out". We have been with several people as they went through a divorce and there was nothing easy about it. Marriage does take work and is not always easy, but the rewards are well worth it.

When I was younger, my idea of marriage was simply to find the right person, marry him and live happily ever after. The End. Now that I'm older and much wiser, I have come to realize that getting married is actually just the beginning.

As our title suggests, marriage is work. It doesn't magically happen on its own without any effort on your part. I have found that there is never a time in marriage, no matter how long two people have been together, when they can lay back and think, "There...we have made it this far, the work is done." Marriage can't be put on automatic pilot. Today, Mark and I are very different from the 18-year-old kids we were when we got married. It would be unrealistic of us to think that the thoughts, plans and ideals we had when we were 18, would continue to work for our relationship during the last 40 years without adjustments along the way. As we have changed and grown as individuals, so has our relationship. We have never assumed that because we had made it 5 years, or 10 years or just passed a major hurdle with no scars, that tomorrow was going to follow suit. Marriage takes work. Marriage is a living thing and it needs constant attention to grow and adapt to our changing lives. While the work is being done, the "Happily ever after" happens, one day at a time.

Mark

I've been trying to learn more about wines lately and have been reading several books on the subject. What I have found is that everyone has the "right" way to experience wine. Some will tell you to let the wine breathe, while other's tell you it doesn't matter one iota if it is opened before serving. One book has a lengthy section about what wines should be served with which foods. And of course, totally contradicting that book, there is one which has the exact opposite information. My favorite book, and the one I think has been most helpful to me, has been a very simple book. This connoisseur says, "This is what I think, not necessarily what you should think. It works for me and hopefully you will get something from this book, but it is not the only way."

I've always been a little leery of people preaching to me with the "my way or the highway" theory. Whether it is religion or wine tasting, I'd like to think there are more ways than one to be successful at something. I feel that way about our book. Jeanine and I have a lot to share with you about what has been helpful to us in keeping our years of marriage happy and healthy. I suggest you

13

read our book as a guide, or a blueprint, realizing that although it has worked for us, it is certainly not the only way to achieve a happy marriage. Don't be afraid to reshape our ideas to fit your needs. Because we are all different people with different ideas, no one formula is going to work for everyone. Wouldn't marriage be simple if that were true? But it's not. Take our ideas and suggestions and stretch them, customize them, and rewrite them to fit your needs. Our wish is that you can create your own set of guidelines by using the basic ground rules we have found helpful in the 40 years of our marriage.

WORKSHEET

What is my definition of marriage?

_____

_____

_____

_____

_____

_____

How have my experiences with divorce affected
my attitude toward marriage?

_____

_____

_____

_____

What are some unrealistic views of marriage we
might have?

_____

_____

_____

_____

The Perfect Marriage

THE PERFECT MARRIAGE

A successful marriage requires falling in love many
times, always with the same person.
Mignon McLaughlin

As we have mentioned, the perfect marriage does not exist, all the time. There are perfect moments during a marriage, and times when you don't think it can get any better, but to assume this blissful feeling is going to last without continuing to work on the marriage, is not a good formula for a lasting marriage. If someone tries to tell you there is such a thing or how to achieve one, they are not being honest with themselves or you. A perfect marriage implies an end result; a finished product which goes against our theory that marriage is an ever changing, ever growing living entity. Marriage is a verb, not a noun.

Although there is no perfect marriage, there is a still a big difference between a marriage and a good marriage. Many people have been married for years, but can't tell you the last time they had a meaningful conversation. Some couples evaluate their marriage by the length of their union. Being unhappily married for 25 years is not a good marriage, it is an endurance test. If you are going to be together, why not enjoy it? Life is too short to be miserable for the rest of it.

We think a good marriage is an ongoing process of growing, changing and learning. Realizing that both partners are going to grow as individuals over time, helps us in understanding and accepting that marriage will also be ever changing. This can be good. Changing and growing together is better. When you are not aware of the differences happening around you, you will be surprised to wake up one morning and find your spouse is not the same person you married. It may seem to have happened overnight, but change is a gradual thing.

While change is a constant companion to a marriage, there are some things that shouldn't change. The basic ingredients or constants that should always be present and counted upon are the foundation pieces for a good marriage.

We have found several basic ground rules that serve as the glue holding us together during the good and the bad times. Every marriage has their own brand of glue and we all need to customize our rules to work for us, but these are some basic assumptions we can count on from each other.

Commitment

The desire of both partners to be with each other for the rest of their lives is commitment. It means not having the option of quitting when things get rough, or fat, or poor or boring. Too many people get married with the idea that marriage is constant bliss and when it isn't, they feel the marriage is a failure and quit. Commitment is an agreement to stick with it through thick and thin. This sounds pretty basic, but you'd be surprised at how many people haven't really consciously thought about this. Two people who plan to be married their entire lives need to be sure that this is what they want and are ready to follow through.

Honesty

You are only fooling yourselves if you are not being honest with your partner. Honesty needs to be there from the smallest things to the biggest things, and all "things" in between. If little white lies slip by, it is just a matter of time before you're comfortable with the big ones.

Trust

Trust is unfortunately one of those things you either have or don't have. If you don't have it, there is usually a reason from past experience. We have seen people develop trust over the years where they had not previously been able to, so it's a "Good Marriage Ingredient" that can be worked on if not there at present. The best advice is not to lose someone's trust in you to begin with.

Respect

Respect will often times takes the place of love when it is temporarily absent in a marriage. Keep in mind that even a good marriage between two people consists of falling in and out of love with each other many times over the years. During those "out of love" times, respect can be a bridge to the next falling in love stage, or act as the filler until the love returns.

Personal Growth

It is as important to grow on an individual basis as well as on a couple level. Just as a good marriage changes and develops into new shapes and forms, so should each person in his or her own unique way. Much of the respect that is needed to get us through the hard times come from the individual growth that has gone on throughout the marriage.

Compromise

One of the skills necessary to a good marriage is compromise. When one person is making all the decisions, you have a dictatorship, not a marriage. Learning to compromise means that you will not always have it "your way", understanding that your turn is coming! Compromising means both people making concessions to improve the whole. It does not mean giving up your individuality or not standing up for your principles. It does mean, in certain areas, giving in a little.

Work

A good marriage does not come without work. Emotional work. It is working on yourselves as individuals and together as a couple. It is taking time from the fun things about marriage to work on the weak spots that come up. Just like anything else that is growing and changing, a marriage needs to be maintained and cared for with effort.

Sense of Humor

Ya gotta have fun! Somewhere, between the serious talks, the passionate feelings, the growing and changing, you just have to laugh! If it's not fun, what is the point?

As we try to blend the beliefs we have in common, like those mentioned above, with the differences we have, we all stumble occasionally along the way. But a good marriage can recover by acknowledging the problem and working on it. When we stumble, we can realize that we are human, maybe even see a little humor in the situation and give it the energy it needs, nothing more. Our other option is to pretend it didn't happen. Shoving it under the carpet where it can hide and grow is asking for trouble down the line. There really is no such thing as a perfect marriage. But a good marriage under constant remodeling and repair, is not only possible, but also fun.

Jeanine

It gives me confidence and support to know that Mark and I both agree on these points. Not only because they help us through our marriage but we both believe in them. I know that Mark is, for example, honest with me because that is who he is, not who he thinks he should be to keep our marriage going. These points all seem to feed on each other for me. Honesty creates trust; trust creates respect, and so on. Knowing that we both are working with the same set of rules assures me that there are going to be fewer surprises down the road. There will always be bumps in the road and a major pothole here and there, but I think because we're both on the same page, we see them coming and are more prepared.

Mark

In my opinion, a good marriage is one that nurtures and supports both people involved. It is a good marriage that acknowledges and nourishes the differences between the two partners. I see Jeanine's and my differences as one of our biggest strengths. We have many differences that compliment each other. For example...I'm an early riser. I go to bed early and get up at the crack of dawn. Jeanine, the night owl, stays up late and sleeps late. This gives us both time to ourselves and creates our own space that we talk about later in the book. (It does however make for tough vacations!) I have every moment of our vacation planned from 7 am on, but she prefers to relax. Can you imagine? We also have differences that aren't so complimentary to each other. After we spent a lot of wasted time and energy trying to change each other, we've realized that accepting these differences and working around them create a good marriage. I am quick to anger and quick to say I'm sorry. Jeanine is slow to anger and even slower to say I'm sorry! I'm not going to change Jeanine's makeup, nor will she change mine. We have adapted a little here and there in that I try not to be so quick with my reactions and Jeanine has learned to vent a little along the way, but for the most part, neither one of us have budged on this issue. Instead, Jeanine has learned to take my negative reactions with a grain of salt and I have learned that when Jeanine blows up about some supposed little thing, it is really a compilation of small angry moments built-up over the last 3 months.

WORKSHEET

What are some of our differences?

_____

_____

_____

_____

_____

_____

How do I feel about accepting those differences?

_____

_____

_____

_____

_____

What are the most challenging differences between us?

_____

_____

_____

_____

Starting Out

Start

STARTING OUT

*Learning to live with and love others requires skills
as delicate and studied as those of the surgeon, the
master builder and the gourmet cook, none of whom
would dream of practicing each profession without
first acquiring the necessary knowledge. Still, we
fragile, ill equipped humans plow ahead, forming
friendships, marrying, raising families with few or
no actual resources at hand to meet the
overwhelming demands.*
                                    Leo Buscaglia

Ideally, we all start out with the tools and the
knowledge needed to make a good marriage. Unfortunately,
most of us begin our marriages with this unrealistic idea of
what marriage will be like.

Most of us aren't aware that we don't have a good
marriage until we've been in the relationship anywhere from a
few years to several, but like they say, "Better late than never!"
So, even if you've been married 20 years, there's no time like
the present to "Start Out", to take the first step of having a good
marriage.

What made a good foundation for our marriage was that
we were away from home and family right off the bat. Mind
you, it was not our idea so we really can't take the credit for

being so smart and worldly at 18 years old, but in looking back, we see that when the Navy sent us off to Spain the day after our marriage, they did us a favor. We saw ourselves as being ripped away from our home and families, but in hindsight, realize it was a great bonding time for us and helped in cementing our marriage from the start.

For newlyweds just starting their lives together, getting away from home, families and all previous strings allow the two to define who they are as a couple. To get away geographically, physically and mentally and to develop as a couple who have only each other to rely on and support, can create a deep bond. Living around family can be wonderful and eventually it's a great idea, but when you're first married, take time to know each other without the influences and back up of the family. When we got married and left our families and familiar surroundings, we had no choice but to look to each other for support. When we hit the rough spots, Mom and her house were not conveniently nearby to run to and a best friend wasn't there telling us how unreasonable our spouse was being and how justified we were in our righteousness. We had to solve our own problems and find a style of doing it that worked for *us*, not our parents or our friends. Instead of being ripped away from our "homes", we created our own "home" which was different in many ways than the ones we left. When we returned three years later to those same people, we were a unit, a couple who knew who we were together, and saw ourselves as a family within ourselves and were committed to each other as a couple, before our other roles as son and daughter, sister, and friend. We feel this was an important first step as a couple. We realize that moving to a new location is not an option for most people, but before moving right next door to your mother-in-law, give it some thought.

For oldyweds (and we use this term respectfully) it is not as easy to "start out" fresh, when you've been walking the same path for years. Take some time to think about how you and your spouse define yourselves as a "unit". How do relatives, friends, and children influence and interfere with your commitment to each other as a couple? Does your mother's opinion hold more weight than your spouses? Is your friend the one you share your feelings with, rather than your spouse? It's not too late to change your priorities.

Being married is being a unit. We don't advise being attached at the hip or alienating yourselves from everyone around you. The root of your marriage is made up of two people, and the outgrowth from that root (relationships with family, interaction with friends etc.) can be enhanced from the strength of the root rather than be pulled on by those

33

relationships stressing the root. A solid foundation makes the marriage secure enough that it is not threatened or negatively influenced by outside relationships.

To be married is to make a commitment of putting each other's feelings before family and friends. To think about how your actions will affect your spouse, is to put them first. If there's any doubt, *ask them.* Don't assume anything.

Many people are married for years and have never sat down and talked about what they expect from marriage. Pre-marriage counseling is a great idea and many couples find out that they expect totally different things from marriage and either solve the problems before they begin their marriage, or even cancel the wedding which beats the heck out of divorce! It's never too late to talk about your expectations of marriage. What is acceptable? Where are the boundaries? Sit down and make a list or a description of what you want your marriage to be, then exchange your lists and talk about it. You may have been working for ten years at making your marriage work, but if both of you are working toward two different goals; don't be surprised that you haven't reached them.

Some questions you might ask each other, depending on your stage in marriage:

What do I see us doing, where will we be living, etc. in 10 years? 20 years?

What are your most serious doubts about this marriage?

Can married couples be each other's best friends?

Are you my best friend? Why? Why not?

Will we have children? How many? Will we both work when children come?

What age do you see us retiring and what will we do then?

Who will handle the finances in our marriage?

Where does spirituality fit into our lives?

How close do we want to be to our families? (Geographically and emotionally).

Do we agree on budget allotments?

As the marriage continues through the years, keep a check on the goals. Are you headed on the right course? Are your goals still the same after 5 years? Do you need to change your goals? Maybe your individual goals have changed and need to be discussed. There has to be a balance of give and take in this relationship of two.

When things aren't going right, *speak up!!* It's dangerous to assume your mate knows what you're thinking. None of us are mind readers. When your spouse is going out three or four times a week to the gym and you think it's too much, talk about it. It isn't fair to a spouse to have him or her guessing at the reason for your anger. Sulking, not speaking or shutting someone out does absolutely nothing but create anger and hurt in the marriage. Give the marriage a chance by getting the real issue out in the open and talking about it. If you are going to be angry, at least know *what* you're angry about! Learn how to communicate right from the beginning.

A good start to a marriage gives it a fair chance. Beginning a marriage is an adjustment in itself without adding unnecessary problems. Start with a clean slate and grow from there. If you are not newlyweds, start where you are. Turn the page and start a new chapter.

Jeanine

When we started out, there were no pre-counseling classes or "how to" classes, we were just pretty much expected to know how to be "married" from either watching how our parents reacted to each other or how June and Ward Cleaver lived their life on the television screen! I saw myself in a cute little apron happily cooking in my perfect little house surrounded by a white picket fence. Mark would come home from work (always happy and having a kiss on the cheek for me) expecting a martini and his slippers waiting for him. Whoa! What a reality check we had. Imagine our surprise when I realized I didn't even know how to cook, much less like it. We could have saved a lot of negative energy had we sat down and discussed what we thought marriage would be. I also think if we had been more aware of the realities of marriage as opposed to the unrealistic "happily ever after" fairy tale, we would have been better prepared. To go into a marriage expecting constant bliss, is setting yourself up for a huge disappointment. I think there are so many false expectations going into marriage that have been put out by the media, that we aren't being honest with ourselves about what marriage is going to be like and therefore are disillusioned and disappointed when we find our real life marriages not holding a candle to the perfect ones we see and fantasize about in print and on films. I love a romantic book or movie, but I have to realize that it is a fantasy. To expect

Mark and I to be on cloud nine all the time based on what I see on a movie screen is not realistic and to think that we have a bad marriage because it doesn't compare to the unrealistic version is not being fair to your marriage. It doesn't stand a chance against the fairy tale.

A lot has happened between our newlywed days and now. The women's movement, poverty, maturity and reality set in. We are so very different than those two young people with stars in their eyes, (thank God). We have not only grown up together but we've grown together in the process.

Start out with a reality check. Know what to expect from a marriage and from your spouse. Let your spouse know what to expect from you. It shows consideration and respect for each other and your marriage.

Mark

The first step of any major goal is a tough one and marriage is no different. The "wedded bliss" moments become further and fewer between as the reality of marriage sets in. The stress of having a "perfect marriage" to show to friends and relatives puts pressure on an already tentative first step in which you are getting to know the "real" person you married.

The level we start at during the first stage of marriage is not very deep. The stars in our eyes keep us from noticing the reality of the situation. A good marriage really gets to work when two people get away from the outside layer of each other and start digging deeper into the levels of emotions and feelings. The labor of marriage begins when you see the other person in the new light of reality.

Preparing yourself for the reality of marriage is a good idea. Like Jeanine said, that wasn't something that was available or common when we got married, so we jumped in the water without having any idea how to swim or how cold the water might get. Although we eventually figured it out, it would have been a lot easier if we had had some guidance and realistic expectations about what marriage consisted of.

When we first get married, we may think we are like a matched set, but eventually, we find there are many differences. Understanding those differences and respecting them is part of the adjustment period. We strive for equality among the sexes, yet we can't deny the differences of men and women, let alone two individuals. When we become man and wife, there is a part of us that feels that we have found our "other half" to make us complete and we relax with a happy sigh, when in reality, the work is just beginning.

WORKSHEET

Answer the questions on page 35.

_____

_____

_____

_____

_____

_____

_____

_____

_____

_____

_____

_____

_____

_____

_____

_____

_____

_____

_____

Commitment

COMMITMENT

Unless commitment is made, there are only
promises and hopes; but no plans.
Peter Drucker

"A long lasting and happy lifetime together", is what you are wished when you marry. The good news is that it is not just a wish, it can happen. It requires both communication and commitment. Communication pretty much covers the "happy" part of the wish, while commitment is usually what keeps the "long lasting" part of the wish going. Commitment isn't usually called upon during the happy times; it is during the not so happy times that it is needed.

Commitment is a word that seems to have gone out of marriage. People are getting married with the attitude of "lets see how it works out." Divorce seems to be an option for unhappy marriages. When we got married we didn't really think about divorce being an option. At the time, in 1969, divorce wasn't as common as it is in today's society. Both of our parents had been married forever as well as most of our friend's parents. Because it wasn't all around us, our expectations were different from couples in marriage today.

45

We never expected to get divorced for any reason and it wasn't an option we considered. As society has changed and the divorce rate continues to climb, it has become easier and more socially acceptable to divorce, taking the seriousness out of commitment. The definition of marriage has changed from a lifetime commitment with one person, to a series of monogamous relationships with one or more partners. Many young couples who are married today have divorced parents as examples of what happens to marriage when it doesn't work. Divorce has become the answer to an unhappy marriage.

We realize there are many cases of divorce that are justified and necessary. Physical or emotional abuse, multiple affairs or criminal behavior are a few of many reasons that we would agree that divorce might be the only answer. This is not to say when something unacceptable happens once in a marriage, it cannot be worked out, but there are definitely circumstances where divorce is the wise and safe thing to do. The marriages we are writing about are the ones that have lost their energy and life and in our opinion, are salvageable.

Commitment has become an outdated idea to a lot of us. We are committed as long as it is convenient. Once it is no longer convenient, we lose our desire or ability to be committed. This isn't just in marriage, but life in general. We can see it in our society all around us. Employees who have committed a lifetime to a company suddenly find themselves "let go" over some technicality and are left in a desperate situation. We see it in how athletes honor their contracts. If they aren't happy, or someone else is getting more money, they renegotiate their contract or move to another team. This leads us all to think we can negotiate our contract on all levels. Marriage is a contract, but unlike the athlete, moving to a new team or a new partnership won't necessarily get you what you want. Agreeing to stay with the team you began with and fix the problems is commitment.

We have said before that there is no such thing as a perfect marriage. To believe you are going to achieve one is not only wishful thinking, but damaging to a marriage because you are bound to be disappointed. There are always going to be the occasional bad days no matter how great your marriage is. Commitment has a lot to do with your attitude while going over the bumps. Just being aware that there are going to be some rough times during your marriage will help you get through them. Marriage can be very fragile, as we have all seen while watching marriages dissolve around us, but commitment can be the strength that makes a marriage last.

Commitment is the glue that keeps you together when things are not so lovely in a marriage. Commitment is reminding yourself of a promise you made to each other to stay the course, regardless of the weather. Commitment is cheering for your marriage even though the odds seem to be very much against it. Commitment is standing by your spouse (whom you may not even bear to look at for the moment) and know that you will get through this together and be stronger for it in the end.

The grass is always greener on the other side of the fence and it is no different in marriage. Most of the time we are very happy and appreciative of being married to each other. On the other hand, there have been many times during our marriage when we were bored to death with each other, causing us to wonder why we were together and wishing our marriage was like the ones we saw in the movies. Commitment gets you through times like these.

As your marriage continues, you build up your own history. Going through rough periods of your marriage and coming out the other end as a stronger couple because of it, reinforces the justification for your commitment. When we find ourselves in the middle of a "blah" time, or it seems like we're arguing all the time, we don't panic and think "the marriage is over!", we say to ourselves, "Hang in there, you've been here before, you'll work it out, it will pass" and eventually it goes. Sometimes it takes hard work, sometimes it passes on its own but it does eventually get settled. It gets settled due to commitment.

We have learned valuable lessons from other people's experiences that have strengthened our reason for commitment. We've seen so many partners become disillusioned with their marriage because the "bells" stopped ringing or the fun and romance were gone. They didn't realize that happens to *every* marriage. Those little weaknesses that were so "cute" in the beginning are starting to grate on each partner. So instead of working on what they have, they give up on it and they look for it elsewhere. Eventually they find it again, make another "commitment" and after awhile they find that they don't hear "bells" anymore and the cycle continues. There are times when we look at those people with stars in their eyes and feel a bit of jealousy because although we quite often have stars in our eyes for each other, we couldn't call it constant wedded bliss with a straight face. When we see the chaos and unhappiness that usually follows these series of monogamous relationships, we have a better appreciation of what we have and our commitment of keeping it grows stronger. We have learned through the mistakes of others that when we aren't hearing bells, the answer is not to listen for bells with someone else, but to put the effort back into our own marriage until we hear our familiar song.

If you compare the building of a long lasting marriage to the building of a house, you will find many similarities. When we built our first house, we had our favorite and least favorite jobs. The planning, the designing and the decorating were some of our favorite things about building the house. It was fun, exciting and full of promise. The insulation, the clean up and protective staining were some things that were not so much fun, yet we were *committed* to building this house. We had a good foundation poured as well as sturdy walls and because we were committed, we didn't abandon the project when we got to the insulation. That would have been a crazy thing to do. Yet some people think that way when it comes to building their marriage. They have a good foundation, great plans and a life full of promise but when they get to a job they don't like, they abandon the marriage.

Commitment is simply sticking with your marriage through the good, but especially the bad, knowing that you are building a worthwhile project. Knowing that each of you are committed to the marriage and won't bail out on each other when the going gets rough, is a comforting thing to know.

50

Jeanine

The longer we're together the stronger our commitment becomes. As we pass each anniversary, we add equity to our marriage. It has become more valuable to me as the years pass, as we grow and as things change in this world. As each year passes, the more committed we become to preserving this precious tapestry we call our marriage. We have worked very hard to make it what it is and therefore appreciate it. We know it is fragile in some ways,, yet it is strong enough to survive the storms that pass through now and then, and it strengthens every year. I am committed to honoring the promise I made to Mark to be married for life. And since I am committed to being here, it only makes sense to make sure that "here" is a happy place to be. It helps me to know that Mark is beside me in commitment, pulling for our marriage, working just as hard to keep it going in a positive direction. We are a team, with a '"no quit" clause in our contract, committed to making our marriage work now and always.

Mark

Going into marriage with a "let's see how it's going to work" attitude has never made sense to me. When Jeanine and I married, we assumed it was forever. I don't think either of us planned to see how it went.

The "Lets see if it works" attitude is more appropriate for buying something with a thirty day, money-back guarantee, such as an appliance. Unfortunately, marriage doesn't come with a guarantee of thirty days or thirty years. No one will be responsible for guaranteeing the length and strength of your marriage but you. You are the guarantor. You are the one to stand behind what you say. When you promise to "love, honor and cherish", you are the one who is expected to follow through. If things aren't working out, there is no "marriage store" to return to with complaints. If there were, you'd find a mirror posted at the door! You made the promise and the commitment, and you get to fix it.

With the possible exception of abuse or chronic infidelity, most problems can be overcome. Part of your ability to overcome these problems, is being committed to the relationship in the first place. If you know that you are in this relationship for life, you will take better care of it, knowing it will always be with you. If you think of your marriage as a disposable part of your life, it loses its value and importance. We are all aware that there are no guarantees in life, and even with commitment, marriages don't always work. But by having commitment as the cornerstone of your relationship you are giving yourselves the best chance at having a long lasting marriage.

WORKSHEET

What does commitment mean to me?

_____

_____

_____

_____

_____

_____

How does it make you feel knowing your partner is committed to making your marriage work?

_____

_____

_____

_____

_____

_____

_____

_____

Communication

COMMUNICATION

Listening with love does not necessarily mean that
we have to agree, but it does mean listening without
attacking or being defensive.
Gerald Jampolsky and Diane Cirincione

If we were making a list of all the vital parts that made up a good, long lasting marriage, communication would have to be at the top of that list. Communication is necessary to keep all the other vital parts working. Love (physical and emotional), trust, commitment and even our differences need to be met on a communicative level. When we are communicating well, the other parts of our lives go much more smoothly.

So much of the fighting and disagreements in a marriage are due to a lack of communication. Most of the time, neither person is actually sure of what they are fighting about. On the surface, the cause of the friction seems to be about one thing, but if you can learn to communicate correctly, you will find it is usually something entirely different.

If you're not used to communicating effectively, it takes some practice. So many times we have gotten used to "our way" of communicating and it has become a habit over the years, even though it has never been effective and never will be. We've seen couples that clam up and won't talk to each other when they're unhappy with a situation in their marriage. As silly as it sounds, this is their way of communicating. This method is effective to a point, in that their anger is apparent, but the communication stops there and the guessing game begins. "Why are we not talking to each other? What are we angry about?" Before you know it, with a little help from your imagination, this "problem" (which you have *no idea* what it is) has gained a life of its own.

Other couples aren't shy at all about airing their anger as they shout back and forth to each other even though neither one is listening. Their frustration level may be lowered, but the problem never gets talked about or solved.

Needing to be *right* sometimes puts a halt to furthering communication. Most of us want to be right and sometimes that isn't possible in communicating our differences. Being stubborn and digging in with our heels at being right rather than trying to solve the problem without blame, sometimes interferes with our communication.

Most of us have never had a "lesson" on communication so it's not surprising that we aren't very good at it. Just like many other skills we need to survive in life, communication skills need to be learned and practiced. Every couple communicates in different ways. What works great for some, will not work at all for another.

We were married probably 5 or 6 years before we actually learned how to communicate. We reluctantly attended a marriage workshop weekend (it was a gift from a family member) and even though we haven't followed through with daily dialogue over the years, it taught us some very basic rules that we use to this day in making our communication skills work better for us. We also learned how good our marriage can be while communicating correctly and often refer to that time as a measuring device as to how our communication is going now.

There are many methods of learning how to communicate. The marriage workshop was a good match for us, but there are various tools to be had all around you. Colleges, churches and local service groups are a great source for seminars, booklets, counseling and workshops available to you. The main thing is that you learn a method of communication that is comfortable for you and of course, one that is effective for you. If you are uncomfortable or awkward in the way you are communicating, you will avoid communicating at all. Take the information that sits well with you and leave the rest. The important thing is to gather all the information available to you and customize it to your marriage, with the results being a method of communication that works for you. Not everything is going to work for everyone.

Writing has been our best source of communicating. We've suggested this to many couples with great results. When we write our thoughts and feelings down on paper, we are able to take the time to think about what we want to say, write it down, then reread it to make sure that is what we intended to say. We can put the letter away for a period of time, and read it again later to see if we have said all that we wanted to say, or if we've said too much. Writing takes away the pressure of speaking your mind when you haven't given much thought to what you want to say. The beauty of letter writing is that it works well for the writer as well as the recipient. Upon receiving a letter from your spouse, you can take the time to read it, digest it, mentally react to it and reread it several times, allowing yourself to understand what is being said.

We found when we tried to communicate verbally we weren't really saying what we wanted to say or what we felt.

Instead of really listening to what our partner was saying, we were getting our reply ready in our minds and waiting for an opening to jump in and be heard. Neither one of us was hearing each other, and very seldom settled anything, much less communicated in any way. We tend to say things we don't mean and to blurt out anything just to be heard. This is *not* communicating, it is a verbal battle. The more we practiced our communication skills in our writing, the more we found them spilling over into our verbal communication. Our best form of communication is still writing.

There are some basic ground rules that we've agreed to stick to when we are "discussing" anything, which seem to make our communication more effective and meaningful:

Fight Fair:

Don't get down to the level of a child. Childish games like name-calling, back stabbing and just plain immature behavior is a waste of time.

Timing is everything:

Pick a good time to communicate. The minute you see each other in the evening after a long day is obviously not the time to enter into a deep and serious discussion. We've found that setting up a time in advance works best for us. When you set aside a specific time for talking, it also gives your communication the importance it deserves. Picking the right time is not an issue when we are writing to each other because we don't read each other's letters until we are relaxed and open to communication. Another plus for writing!

Be kind:

Don't intentionally hurt your spouse. There are times when this is unavoidable, but to crush your spouse "on purpose for no purpose" is simply being cruel. We all know where the tender areas are in our partners, because at some time, in a softer moment, they have shared personal stories with us about their feelings. To turn around and use that information to hurt them, will not only throw trust right out the window, guaranteeing they will never share with you again, but it does nothing for communication except build a wall.

No judgments on feelings:

An important thing we've carried with us since our

marriage workshop weekend 35 years ago is about feelings. Agree and understand that our feelings can't be helped. We can't judge a feeling as being right or wrong. It is a feeling and whether you agree or disagree with why your spouse should feel a certain way, this is how they feel right now. Understanding this, we can communicate more openly knowing we are not going to be judged about how we feel. Using the same theory, when we express ourselves, we talk a lot about feelings, not blame. To read a note from my spouse that says he feels hurt when I walk away from him as he's talking to me, allows me to feel compassion for him and put myself in his shoes. If he comes from a place of anger (which unfortunately is more acceptable and comfortable in our society) and blames me for making him feel bad when I walk away from him, I feel like I'm being attacked and want to defend myself by attacking in return, or putting up a wall. Either way, it does nothing to further the communication. If you can substitute "I think" for "I feel" in your conversation, you are not describing a feeling, but a thought. For example: "I feel that you are being insensitive" is not a feeling, it is a thought, a judgment against someone. On the other hand to say "I feel hurt when you raise your voice at me" is describing a feeling. In the first statement, you are accusing your spouse of being a certain way, as opposed to the second statement in which you are sharing your feelings, not attacking anyone. Which statement will get you off to a better start at communicating? Which statement would you like to hear coming from your spouse if you were about to have a discussion about a recent argument?

If you take most any situation, remove the anger from it and come from the place of love, you will communicate so much more effectively and peacefully. If you practice looking into the feelings you have, you will usually recognize one of two feelings: Fear or Love. If you can see past the anger to the fear underneath, it is easier to have compassion and understanding. We have seen hurtful, unproductive arguments of ours turn into loving, bonding experiences with just a few of the words rearranged.

Good communication is not just for the purpose of airing your differences about your relationship. Use your good communication skills for meaningful conversation. Communicate about your future plans, your children's problems, your feelings, (good and bad), or about your job. I heard someone saying "You can always recognize the dating couples from the married couples in a restaurant. The dating couples are talking, listening and laughing while the married couples are barely speaking to each other as they observe their fellow diners, which seem to be far more interesting." Sad, but true in many cases. Next time you are out to dinner with your spouse, make an effort to have a *meaningful* conversation. It is said that the average couple communicates with each other for seventeen minutes a day. If this is true for you, at least make those seventeen minutes of communication meaningful ones and you might surprise yourselves by finding that you are looking forward to more talks with your spouse.

Making your relationship with your spouse fun and special comes with learning to communicate about anything. When we open our mouths to speak to each other about anything, we try to apply the basic rules of communication and we can honestly say there is nothing that we cannot talk about to each other. There are not too many people in your lives that you can say this about and it is great to have your lifetime partner be that person.

Jeanine

I tend to be stubborn. (Mark will laugh at the "tend" in that sentence). It may be the Taurus in me or the fact that I like to be right, but for whatever reason, it's a long streak. When we start to disagree on something, I have several choices. I can argue my point until I wear Mark out. I can put up a wall to show Mark I disagree and don't even want to talk about it. I can play mind and word games with Mark all day long and still not accomplish anything positive. Another choice I have is to change my attitude to that of a "grown-up" and apply the rules that we know will work for us, and then simply solve the problem. We still get to air our concerns, hurts and disappointments, but in a kind and loving way.

It saddens me to look back on 40 years of marriage and see the time that we've wasted on ineffective communication. Many times, what could have been a controlled and productive fifteen minute discussion, has turned into days, weeks and even months of putting up walls and defenses to no avail. One would think that after discovering such an obvious working solution, we would automatically apply our "rules" to every diverse subject that came up in our house. One would be wrong. We still have the occasional useless bickering and every now and then it just feels good to be "right" at all costs as my stubborn streak dig its heels in, but for the most part, we stick to the plan that works for us and it makes a huge difference in the quality of our marriage.

Mark

As we have said, communication is possibly the most important aspect of a relationship. I have always struggled with this area. I tend to be one of those people who let things stay inside. Jeanine gets so tired of saying, "What's wrong" and hearing my reply of "nothing", when there is obviously something bothering me. When we finally do talk about the problem, there is a relief from getting it off my chest. Sometimes just saying something out loud makes you realize how insignificant it is. Then, of course, you see it was pointless to be holding all that negative energy inside. In most good working relationships, partners must be able to talk about everything. Talk about the good things too, not just problems. I think we are all a little leery when our spouse says, "We need to talk". If you spend enough time talking with your spouse about your joys as well as your concerns, when you hear "we need to talk" you won't automatically assume you are going to talk about a problem.

WORKSHEET

What is my most comfortable way of communicating?

_____

_____

_____

_____

How do I receive communication best?

_____

_____

_____

_____

How are my listening skills?

_____

_____

_____

_____

What method of communicating would work best for us as a couple?

_____

_____

Common Goals

COMMON GOALS

Love does not consist in gazing at each other,
but looking outward in the same direction.
Antoine de Saint-Exupery

Have you ever noticed how some couples seem to know where they are headed while others are not even on the same path? We have found that setting goals and making a plan for our lives together is the key to getting us headed in the right direction. If we are both headed in a totally different direction, we are not going to end up at the same place.

Common goals that you've made together will be the road map as your marriage continues. As you accomplish the goals you've set, you will feel pride in yourselves and each other as you complete them. Keeping the goals flexible is also important. As we go through marriage, things are constantly changing and we must be ready to change as well. Even though we have a plan, it should be a flexible one, with the ability to change periodically. Just like the highway we drive on everyday, the marriage route has construction along the way and we need to take a detour now and then, eventually getting back on the main road.

73

Sitting down and going over your goals can be a surprising jolt for both of you. You may find your ideas are very different from each other's. Putting your heads together on the major goals and making sure you are both in agreement can lessen the confusion in attaining these.

Of course, your goals will vary depending on the stage of life you are in, but some of the goals we suggest you talk about are these:

Career related plans:

What are our career plans? What do each of us plan to do for a living? How do our individual career plans intertwine with each other? Does either of our career choices require cooperation from the other partner, such as unusual hours, change in location or travel time away from home? Has either of us contemplated changing careers?

Family related goals:

What are our goals as a family? Do we *want* a family? How many children do we want? Who will be the primary caregiver? How much time and effort does each of us plan to put toward a family.

Location:

Where do we want to live? Are we city people or country people? Do our chosen careers give us the option of living where we want? Do we want to live near relatives?

Financial goals:

How do we picture ourselves living? Of course we always see ourselves in the house of our dreams but this is a time to be realistic. Some couples will have jobs that allow them to make a great deal of money, others won't. Teaching, for example, is a noble and wonderful career but not likely to set you up financially for that mansion of your dreams with the ocean view. When setting your financial goals, be realistic. Realize that if you want the mansion, you will be spending a lot more time at work than the teacher in the suburb and less time doing what you enjoy.

Fun:

It's too bad that we have to set a goal to have fun, but we've found that unless we make the plans, make the reservations and pay for the tickets, we end up only talking about "wouldn't that be fun!" What is your idea of a good time? Do you both see yourselves traveling? If so, will you be backpacking or staying at the Ritz. One of you might be surprised to see your accommodations unless you've talked about your plans!

Some of the happiest times in our marriage came when we were working on a specific goal together. We packed up our stuff, our kids and moved to a new location to further our educations. It was one of the poorest times we went through in many ways, yet instead of not getting along because of all the hardships we were going through, we became stronger as a couple because we had a common goal...getting through school and on to better lives for all of us. If we didn't have that common goal, we may have fallen apart from the stresses coming at us from the outside. Our common goal was the light at the end of our tunnel, and when we accomplished that goal we were proud of *us*.

It's always good to have your own personal goals apart from the relationship, but we have found that it's just as important to have common goals threaded throughout the marriage at the same time. It doesn't always have to be such a life-altering goal such as our going to school was. That was a big goal and we had to adjust our lives severely to attain that goal. It's good to have several little common goals as well as big ones. Where you are in your lives will determine the kind of goals you will have. Newlyweds have a common goal of getting ahead and getting roots. Raising kids automatically gives you a common goal. When the kids are gone and you're looking towards slowing down your lives, the common goal might be making retirement plans.

Many times during our years together we have taken a look at our marriage only to find that we have absolutely nothing in common. Our individual lives have gradually gone off in such different directions that we are living in two separate worlds. That is the time to make an adjustment. We sit down and think about what can we do together that we enjoy. If we've been talking about learning a foreign language, we'll sign up for a Spanish class at the community center. Maybe we both could be in better shape so we'll agree to walk every night and lose some weight together. Or maybe you can write a book together! Sometimes, there is absolutely nothing you can find that you'd like to do together, so you bite the bullet and say (to yourself) "Okay, I don't really like to golf, but I will put forth the effort for *us* and play golf once a week with you." Or, "It won't kill me to take the dance classes that my spouse has wanted to do for so long." You will be surprised at the fun you can have trying something new and different.

Whether they are big goals that are life changing or the smaller ones like learning a new skill together, the fact that you have them in common is the important thing. To have things in common amongst busy schedules and lives going in several different directions is sometimes the only glue you have holding your relationship together

Jeanine

We live on an island, away from the city. Many people who live here, who are now parking meter attendants, store clerks and bed & breakfast managers were once "City People." Their lives were made up of high stress, high paying jobs and high maintenance living. Both partners were either at their desks working or in traffic on their way to work most of their waking hours, each thinking that this was the lifestyle their partner wanted. When they started discussing their goals and what was important to them in life, they found their goals had changed since the beginning of their relationship, but they hadn't discussed it with each other. They began setting new goals, with the quality of life becoming a priority, and changed the direction of their path. Today, the former executive is a woodworker, making a fraction of his former salary, but enjoying his life tenfold. The entire family has grown closer and loves their new cabin on the lake. Who knows what they'd be doing today if they hadn't sat down and talked about their goals and how their thinking had changed. As we grow and change personally and as a couple, so do our goals. It's a good idea to review and rewrite your goals now and then and realize that they need to change along with us. The key is having the common goals. "Dropping out" of the city life isn't for everyone, obviously, but we all have "if only" dreams that can

79

become a reality if we are working on it together. `Not only does your dream have a better chance of coming true, but your marriage will grow stronger during the voyage.

Mark

Having common goals is a very important concept, and in many cases difficult. In our case, I am very goal oriented. I like lists and marking things off lists! (I've heard Leo's do this) I like to know exactly where I am headed, even if my concept of where I am going changes tomorrow. Jeanine is more of a "lets wait and see what happens" kind of a person, less goal oriented than myself. She lives her life one day at a time. So, our challenge has been to blend these two very different concepts into one that works for both of us. Our blended concept is to have a plan for our future, which is flexible, yet allows us to live each day as it comes, not waiting for the future plans to pan out before we start living our lives.

WORKSHEET

Make notes on the individual goals mentioned in this
chapter?

_____

_____

_____

_____

_____

_____

_____

_____

_____

_____

_____

_____

_____

_____

_____

_____

_____

_____

Honesty and Trust

HONESTY AND TRUST

Sooner or later, everyone sits down to a plate of consequences.
Robert Louis Stevenson

Honesty and trust are two very big components in a marriage and they usually come as a set. Trusting your partner is knowing that you can count on them to be honest with you. In being honest with your spouse, you are trusting that he or she will respect your freedom to be honest.

Some couples we know want no part of honesty. The old adage "What we don't know, can't hurt us" is their marriage motto. We disagree. What you don't know can not only hurt you, but give that "unknown" much more power than it deserves. When the truth is out in the open and available to both partners, there is nothing to hide or tiptoe around.

The best way to develop honesty and trust in a marriage is from the beginning. Once you have that as a standard and stick with it, there is no reason to doubt the honesty of each other and trust comes about automatically. It is a little harder to achieve complete honesty and trust once it has been abused, but not impossible.

Honesty and trust are not always easy to come by. It is sometimes easier to make up a little lie, or withhold information about something to keep from paying the consequences of some activity. It may be uncomfortable being a "little" dishonest with your partner, and come with some guilt, but with enough practice, it will become more natural and require little thought. Soon, you will be able to lie about the big things with as much ease as you did with the little white lies. Your comfort zone of dishonesty will change and adapt according to your actions.

Your reactions to your partner's honesty will either help or hinder their ability to be honest with you. If you keep in mind that although what your spouse is telling you may be hurtful, they did have the option of keeping it to themselves or lying about it. If you react in a violent and negative manner to what your spouse is honestly sharing with you, you are discouraging them from being honest with you the next time. After all, why would they want to create a reaction like this? This doesn't mean that you don't have the right to have negative or angry thoughts about the issue brought up and discuss the consequences; it is the reaction to the truth that we are talking about. Respect and honor the act of honesty your partner has shared with you.

Jeanine

Honesty is a huge thing with me, maybe because I'm honest to a fault. (Could there be such a thing?) I don't think I could live with a man who wasn't honest. There is something about someone trying to fool you with lies that makes me feel cheated, humiliated and a page behind everyone else. It is a total lack of respect for someone to lie to you, no matter what their reason. They are, in effect, saying "I will decide what you will or will not know because you can't handle the truth." What a slap in the face. A lie, gives an ordinary statement, a power it didn't possess before.

Years ago, when we had been married a few years, I was cleaning out a closet and came across a stack of "girlie" magazines. I was surprised because I didn't know Mark read those kind of magazines but beyond that, I was angry about the lie. By hiding the magazines from me in the top of a closet, he was keeping a secret, and in my mind, he was not being honest. I didn't care if he read the magazines. I would have bought them for him if he wanted, but the issue was the fact that he hid them and made them into something more powerful and negative than they were. The lie, or omission, turned a magazine filled with beautiful women's bodies into something nasty and to be hidden. Keeping secrets, no matter how small you think they are, is the beginning of a dishonest relationship. There is a peace in knowing that there are no secrets between you

87

and your spouse. There is also a satisfaction of knowing that there is nothing you can't share with each other, no matter how good or bad. There is great comfort in knowing you have that with your partner for life.

Mark

Jeanine and I have always been very honest with each other and because of that, we have no reason to mistrust each other. There have been many things that have happened to each of us over forty years that would have been easier to not make mention of, rather than talk about them honestly. Some of these things have been hurtful to talk about and admit, but by sharing our honest feelings, we have gotten through some hard times together with a new respect for our relationship and how well it works. The fact that someone is being honest with you when they have a choice to keep it a secret or hide it away gives you respect for that person because it takes courage to be honest. There is an appreciation of that openness that grows in your relationship when you have an honest one. When you are honest with each other, you know there are no surprises coming down the road and there is a comfort in knowing that your relationship has a solid base and is not based on lies or half-truths. It is something you can count on.

WORKSHEET

Do you trust your partner? If not, why not?

_____

_____

_____

_____

Can you be honest with your partner? If not, why not?

_____

_____

_____

_____

What is your reaction when your partner is uncomfortably honest with you?

_____

_____

_____

_____

_____

Creating Your Own Space

CREATING YOUR OWN SPACE

*Love is the free exercise of choice. Two people
love each other only when they are quite capable of
living without each other but choose to live with each
other.*
M. Scott Peck

Creating your own space in a marriage goes hand in hand with keeping your own identity. Sometimes, your own "space" comes about naturally. In our case, as Mark has mentioned, one of us is a night person and the other a morning person, so we have our own quiet time and space without really working on it. But most of the time, you have to schedule your own space, just as you would for any other appointment that is valuable. When both partners are aware of the need for each others time alone, it is easier to develop that time without reading anything into it, such as "You want to be away from me?" It's not that you need to be away from your partner, it's that you need time to be by yourself, for yourself.

What do you *do* with your own space? There are several things you can do with it. Sit in a corner and read a book without guilt, write in a journal, go fishing, soak in a hot bath with candles and good music, take a drive by yourself, take a big lunch and go hiking, go golfing. Do whatever *you* want to do. What do you *not* do with your own space? Catch up on work that needs to be done, spend time doing what others want you to do, feel guilty about taking this time for yourself. Get the picture? It's a nice time taken just for you.

To take time out for yourself and do something that is just for you is a luxury not many couples take for themselves. It's not that there is a "problem" in the marriage or that you are driving each other crazy, it is just a time when you feel like being away from your spouse and marriage. for no particular reason, taking time for yourself and doing it without guilt, pressure or reason.

Couples taking separate vacations cause some people to gasp. It's a fun thing to do now and then. Our friend John is an accountant who spends most of his days and nights at the office during the month of April, while his wife and daughters take off for a week of camping. In August, John who is a sailing fanatic took a vacation and went to Australia by himself on a guided sailing trip. It doesn't matter where you go, just that you go and remind yourself that there is an individual you that is still alive and well. Let the avid golfer spend a week of nonstop golfing on the coast and the beachcomber search for treasures all week long on beaches.

Both will enjoy themselves with no guilt and come back renewed and anxious to share their experiences.

Creating a space just for you is not going somewhere that you can be away from everything, but a time to be *with* yourself. It's a time for you to get back in touch with your own individuality. A time to touch base with that person who isn't a spouse, or parent or associate. You don't necessarily have to be alone in the space you've created. It might be spent with a group or a good friend, but the point is that it is time set aside to be spent on your own well being without any explanation or guilt required.

So make some plans for a weekend at the shore by yourself, an afternoon of sailing or a time spent with friends. You owe it to yourself, each other and your marriage to take the time and effort to create this space.

Jeanine

Years ago when our kids were small and money was tight, my friends and I took one weekend a year and just took off to a cabin in the woods. It became etched in stone as "The Girl's Weekend." The dads or grandparents took care of the kids and we had a weekend with no responsibilities or cares. It doesn't sound like much time, but when the weekend was over we all felt renewed. What we did every year varied but it always involved doing things we didn't normally allow ourselves the time to do. We indulged in deep and meaningful discussions, some confessions, some tears, lots of giggles and silliness, but all of it a part of letting off steam. By the end of the weekend, we were missing our kids and husbands and having more appreciation for them than when we left. We always jokingly referred to it as our "Therapy Weekend" but I think that was closer to the truth than we realized. Depending on your stage, age and finances in life, your opportunities for creating "space" will vary. Now that the "girls" are over 50 with no kids and less responsibility, they take off to Hawaii for a week to themselves. The problems and worries are different than they were 35 years ago, but it is still needed therapy.

Mark

Having your own space gives you freedom to just be you, the individual rather than you the spouse or parent. We all need time to ourselves. In our situation, Jeanine goes to where she was raised in Alaska for a few weeks to be with family and friends. It is a time for me to just hang out without feeling I should be doing something else. I have the chance to watch movies, read books, and have a drink of good scotch without feeling guilty. (Jeanine has this look she gives me when I drink hard liquor and it takes all the fun out of it.) I've been known to spend the entire day at the golf course. It is a time to just be me. We also have time to ourselves on a regular basis with the schedules we keep. The early morning hours are mine and the late night hours are Jeanine's. I have time to myself in the morning to read, write and kick around in my space. Jeanine can be found knitting or working on a craft late into the night. Even though we are trying to make time for us together, we also need time for us alone.

WORKSHEET

How does it make you feel when your partner wants time alone?

_____

_____

_____

_____

_____

Are you able to take time to yourself without feeling guilty? If not, why not?

_____

_____

_____

_____

When is the last time you and your partner have each had time for yourselves alone?

_____

_____

_____

_____

Taking the Temperature
Of Your Marriage

TAKING THE TEMPERATURE
OF YOUR MARRIAGE

*It is only possible to live happily ever after
on a day to day basis.*
                        Margaret Bonnano

Too many couples think their work has ended when they get to a certain point in their marriage. It might be a ten-year anniversary or getting past a problematic six-month period, that gets them to thinking that they can make it through anything from now on. They are happily in love, have all their problems ironed out and look forward to a smooth sailing relationship from here to eternity without a problem in sight. This is what makes a great movie script, not a great marriage.

Like anything that is growing, changing and constantly being tested, a marriage needs regular maintenance check-ups. Marriages need to be graded periodically with a "How are we doing test?" and adjusted accordingly. It's unfortunate but true that our cars receive better maintenance checkups than most marriages today.

For whatever reason, it seems the wife is usually the one who is the first to notice that things aren't going so smoothly or becomes unhappy with the way the relationship is going. A friend of ours was in shock when his wife asked him for a divorce. They never had a fight the whole time they had been together and because of this, he assumed they had a marriage made in heaven. Most husbands we know think that if there isn't fighting or arguing going on in their homes, they must have a good marriage. There is a lot more to a good marriage than "not fighting".

When things are going really good between you and your spouse, there is a feeling of ease and contentment that you get comfortable with. You will also know the minute you walk into each other's space if there is a problem. (We're happy to say that men *do* get better at recognizing this as a great relationship grows) The worst thing you can do when being asked what is wrong at this time, is to say "nothing." We all say "nothing" for several different reasons. We think we are making a major ordeal over a minor thing (which may be true, but *talk* about it anyway). You may think your spouse will think you are silly, petty or exaggerating for thinking the way you do (which may also be true, but again, *talk* about it). Some of us want to be begged to talk about things ("If you really love me, you will spend more time trying to find out why I am unhappy. *And,* if you really knew me you'd *know* why I am angry so now you'll just have to *guess* until you get it right!) Life is too short for game playing. *Talk* about it. When you recognize the first degree of discomfort in your marriage, get it out in the open. Don't give a small problem the opportunity to become a huge one

It may be as simple as finding out that one of you is just "in a bad mood" or "had a bad day." Letting your spouse know that this is the reason for your "mood" will end the bad vibrations immediately, as opposed to giving it power by keeping quiet and assuming it's more serious. Sharing your bothersome thoughts with your spouse, such as, "You hurt my feelings yesterday when you blew up at me," can take the steam out of that hurt before it blows into a bigger issue and puts a wedge between you both. We find when we don't talk about things that are interrupting our "good feeling" about our relationship, they end up getting more of our negative energy than they deserve. Lack of communication causes our imaginations to come up with ideas that aren't even close to the truth about why we're uneasy.

We have found that it is so much easier to talk about little problems we see and adjust things along the way than to wait until those little things turn into big things which are harder to talk about and to fix. Remember that marriage is a party of two, and both partners need to be constantly taking the temperature of the marriage. Allowing this task to be the

105

responsibility of one person isn't sharing the maintenance portion of the marriage. You both need to be watching for pitfalls and rocks along your path.

Marriages don't go bad overnight. One little thing after another gets added to the "problem pile" without being talked about and before you realize it, the pile is so big, you don't know where to start. At this point, it may seem like a hopeless cause. If you solve one little problem at a time, as it comes up, you will be fine-tuning your marriage everyday and keep it functioning at the best it can be.

Jeanine

I've learned that anything worth having usually takes some time, attention and caring on my part. I liken the maintenance of our marriage to my piano playing. I love to play the piano and I love to play it well. I do not enjoy practicing pieces, running the scales or finger exercises, but I know that if I put in the time, I will be happy with the results of my playing. If I have a particularly hard piece, it takes more time and attention to figure out, just like any rough spot in our marriage. I've also found that the longer I'm away from the piano, the harder I have to work to get back to the level I was at and the more excuses I can find to avoid sitting down and getting to work at the piano. Our marriage is not that different in that if we ignore it for awhile, don't practice communicating, or don't check out how we're doing, we find it harder to get back into the smooth comfortable pace we had when we were paying attention to our marriage. The longer we go without that contented feeling of meshing together as a couple, the longer and harder it seems to get us moving in that direction. If we take a small amount of time every day or week to check out how we're doing as a loving couple and change our course accordingly, we save hours and days of unhappy and uncomfortable backtracking to the source of our problem. The lesson to be learned is this: If you want to make beautiful music together, ya gotta

Practice! Practice! Practice! (SO corny......but I couldn't help myself.)

Mark

John F. Kennedy said, "The time to repair the roof is when the sun is shining." These words can aptly be applied to the relationship of marriage. Just as any structure that is in need of maintenance and repair, the structure of your marriage needs to be looked at on a regular basis for wear and tear. Prevention is the key to keeping a well-maintained relationship. Keeping your eyes and ears open to problems creeping up are essential to keeping a strong marriage in good health. From past experiences in your relationship, you know the feeling when things are going well in all areas of your marriage. You know how it feels to have a close and loving relationship with your spouse. You know what a healthy 98.6 on the thermometer feels like. Use that knowledge from past experience as a guide when checking up on your marriage. Knowing what a good marriage feels like helps you monitor your relationship as you go along. I know when I walk into a room if Jeanine and I are doing well, just from the "vibes" we give to each other. If there is a tension between us, I can feel it and so can Jeanine. That "what did I do" feeling is a good sign to pay attention to (and get to the bottom of) before it becomes a problem. To make repairs and adjustments to your relationship "when the sun is shining" is much easier than to wait until you have a hurricane brewing to try and make things better.

WORKSHEET

What are the first signs in your marriage that things aren't going as well as they could be?

_____

_____

_____

_____

_____

_____

What do you do about those signs?

_____

_____

_____

_____

_____

How do you deal with those negative vibrations in the room?

_____

_____

Change of Plans

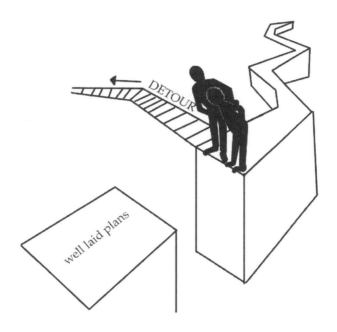

CHANGE OF PLANS

Change is not made without inconvenience,
even from worse to better.
Richard Hooker

No one can get through life without change. It is one
of the few things that are guaranteed. Just when you think
that things are running along smoothly in a marriage, along
comes change and you are forced to balance the new factor
into the equation. Some changes are planned for and
expected, while others come out of nowhere, when you least
expect them. How you deal with these surprises in your life
as a couple will directly affect the even flow of your
marriage.

Probably the most common and drastic change most
married couples face is having children. If you've had a
child, you know the meaning of change. You can plan for a
child, know he or she is coming and you still have no idea
how much your lives are going to change until that little
bundle of energy graces your doorstep. Your plans and their
plans are sometimes very different and the more you can
work as a team in raising children, the easier it will be.

It seems that about the time you have figured out the
"key to raising children", they go onto a new stage and you

are at square one again without instructions. When raising our kids, we felt torn in all different directions when various problems came up. Each of us had our own ideas about how to handle a situation and our theories were very far apart. We had to move away from our differences and zero in on what we had in common. What we *did* have in common was finding a solution to the problem. When we found we were both in the same boat, we began to row in the same direction, combining our ideas and solving the problems together. Working as a team eliminated the added stress of dealing with each other's crisis and left us to put our full attention and energy towards dealing with our kid's challenges, not on differences of our opinions. Of course, once we solved a particular problem, they served us up with a new dilemma and we were back at the drawing board.

Planned changes, such as having children, relocating, or taking on a new job, give you the opportunity to prepare for the event and make the adjustment a little less traumatic. Unexpected changes are not so neatly wrapped up. Changes that come from out of nowhere are the ones that require taking out all the tools you have gathered in your "marriage maintenance kit" and putting them to use.

Friends of ours were sailing along smoothly in the good life they had created when he unexpectedly lost his job in this failing economy. They were stunned and felt quite a jolt at how their lives were about to drastically change. The new cars, the vacations, and the private schools had to go. Instead of letting this huge unexpected change create more turmoil by affecting their marriage, they worked together to solve the problem. Their lives have changed to a much simpler life and they are doing great. It's been a challenge, but one they took on with the tools they had acquired along their path and actually enjoy the new life.

Other friends retired not too long ago, after careful planning on their parts. They had great visions of traveling across the United States and maybe eventually over to Europe. Within a few months after their retirement celebrations, one of their parents began the early stages of Alzheimer's disease and the other had a stroke and needed constant care. Obviously, their plans have changed. The worries, fears and disappointment they are facing now, are putting stress on themselves as individuals as well as their marriage. Each of them is giving so much energy to their parents, they have little left to give to the marriage. Having had a well-maintained marriage before these events, are helping them cope with their new challenges as a couple.

We never know when our lives are going to change drastically. Accidents and illnesses have an effect on

117

everything in our marriage, not just the physical aspects. Your financial situation may change due to unexpected bills and loss of income. Emotionally, you find yourselves stressed to the limit. Relationships are tested in areas that have never been visited before.

We have seen marriages torn apart by tragedy, while others have grown closer than they ever thought possible. What makes the difference?

Using your communication skills in understanding how each partner feels is a must. Realizing that you are both hurting inside and need each other's support now, maybe more than ever, is a key to getting through the situation together. Putting blame on each other, going over the "what ifs" and "you should haves" will get you nowhere. Compassion, patience, and honesty will cement your commitment to get you through the crisis. If you have been practicing these skills all along in your relationship, they will come easy and naturally. On the other hand, expecting rusty tools that haven't been used in months to kick into action under times of stress is not a reasonable assumption. Using your marriage skills on a daily basis creates a habit. You will appreciate this habit when you find yourself in need of help and find these familiar tools to be a part of your relationship.

Jeanine

After about 8 years of marriage, we had bought a house, had two children and were getting along with our plans for the future. Mark worked at a grocery store while attending college full time and I had a part-time job at an insurance company. Our lives were running fairly smoothly and on the schedule we had mapped out for ourselves. Our son Scott was 6 years old and Laura was just a baby of 6 months.

One sunny summer day, Scott had just bought a Popsicle from the ice cream man and started crossing the street to our house, when a speeding motorcycle veered around the bend and hit him. We thank God he was not killed. He did, however, spend a month in the hospital, the summer in a body cast and several months recuperating with a walker and crutches before he healed completely. In that six-month period, many changes took place. I quit my job and spent a lot of time at the hospital. Mark rearranged his schedule to work the night shift stocking shelves and took a quarter off from school. He spent his days at the hospital relieving me, working at home taking care of Laura and pitching in with the household duties of cooking, cleaning and laundry. Scott became our number one priority. As each day passed with new reports from doctors and labs, our emotions were stretched tighter than a drum. Our marriage was on the back burner with no

119

attention being paid to the simmering pot. During stressful times like these, if there are cracks in a marriage to begin with, you can bet they will get larger under stress. Thanks to the regular maintenance of our marriage before the accident, we had a healthy relationship that supported us both during this terrible time. There was no blame, no complaining about the extra work we were both putting in. We both worked at being supportive and helpful to each other for the good of our son. I think if we had entered this incident with a tired and broken down marriage, it would have magnified our marital problems and driven us to different corners.

You never know when you are going to need to pull from the strength of your marriage. Keeping your marriage in top condition at all times will allow you to be able to handle the big changes that unexpectedly enter your lives, as well as enjoying your relationship on a daily basis.

Mark

Change is part of life. It is inevitable. Our lives change for several reasons; we decide to change, a major event forces us to change or we change as we grow to another phase of our lives. Whatever the reason, it happens to all of us. I heard a motivational speaker named Tremendous Jones once, and he said something that has always stuck with me. "You must plan for the future, but *your plan had better be flexible." Change is natural, it is part of the ebb and flow of life, but it doesn't always happen in the way you had it pictured in your mind.*

New adventures can be the most exciting part of life. It can give your life character and fun. We all talk about getting into a routine. Change breaks that routine up. It makes us be more creative.

The first 17 years of our marriage were spent in change, just with the moving we did. We spent time traveling with the military, going to school in various places, and tried new careers before finally putting down roots in our present home. We moved 19 times in 17 years. We don't necessarily suggest that as a way of life, but because of that, we became very adaptable to change. We have learned the art of "flexible planning."

Jeanine is by nature a person who doesn't like change and is very happy with the stability of the nest we have made in the last 20 years. I, on the other hand, thrive on change. I get bored with our routine and want to shake up our lives with new plans and new horizons. Sometimes it has been a challenge to our marriage and relationship. We have worked it out over the years however, by adapting to each others desires. In the early years, Jeanine went with all my ideas to change our lives. She was reluctant, but she would always go along. In the last few years, she has learned to drag her feet or humor me until my desire to change has faded. We

121

both know what is happening and in the end, we both get what we really want. I spend hours planning (which is fun in itself) and Jeanine takes my ideas with a grain of salt, knowing that I am usually just thinking out loud and we are not actually going to sell everything we own and move to Tahiti. Sometimes change just for the sake of change isn't a good idea. I get the fantasy of change and she has learned to know when I am serious about changing our lives, or just traveling in my mind.

Be prepared and let change excite you. It can be fun.

WORKSHEET

What are some unexpected changes that have happened during your relationship? And how did you both handle the change?

_____

_____

_____

_____

_____

_____

_____

_____

_____

What would you have done differently, in hindsight, in dealing with that change?

_____

_____

_____

_____

_____

_____

In The Bedroom

IN THE BEDROOM

The more time you spend making love in your relationship, the better your sex life will be.
Barbara DeAngelis

If we told you that good marriages are made up of couples that have great sex lives, which surpassed the "national average" by leaps and bounds, we would be stretching the truth. Quite a bit. To begin with, we have never found a lasting couple who *hasn't* had some troubles and complaints about the quality and quantity of their lovemaking. In reality, the discontent we hear of from couples, young and old, is usually the same: The men don't "get enough", as the mantra goes, and the women have a headache, a period, PMS (pre *and* post) or are just "not in the mood." Sound familiar? Don't worry, you are in good company. There are more of "us" than there are of "them" who make up those once-a-day sex surveys. The chances of finding a man who complains of having *too* much sex or a woman who just isn't getting *enough* are pretty rare! They are out there, just not everywhere, as you are led to believe.

There is undue pressure put on everyone by comparing themselves to the magazine's "average male" or "average female." Men are having a hard enough time in

127

the bedroom without trying to make sure their wives are having multiple orgasms, like all the other women "out there" and women are feeling guilty because they are not keeping up with the frequency that the "National Average" has deemed to be normal in a relationship. On the other side of the coin, women are reading about how satisfied their peers are and feeling a little left out, whereas men are feeling cheated for only "getting it" once a week. No one is benefiting from the polls except the poll makers. The "national averages" are turning love making into a sport with their ongoing statistics.

Your sexual life is one of the most personal issues in your marriage. Unfortunately, it can also be one of the most problematic issues. Mentally, there is so much happening in our bedrooms, it's a wonder we ever physically get it together and have fun. There are so many emotions bouncing around in our bedrooms and the games that are being played in this room are both positive and negative. Not to mention the power trips, fragile egos, love, guilt, lust, fear, blame and stage fright just to name a few.

First off, we suggest you throw the national average away. Do you know that a survey was done that included 100 couples in which the men's answer to "How often do you and your spouse make love to each other in one month?" was fifty percent higher than the numbers their spouse's gave. Surveys have us believing that our sex lives are pathetically slow. Have you ever read a survey about sex and realized you were *above* average? Most people haven't. If all these people are having so much sex...how come we never talk to one?

There are times in all relationships where sex is very hot. You can remember those well enough. When you first meet and the flirting and teasing begin...there is some nice sex. When you have been away from each other for a time, it is very exciting to rekindle that fire in your bed. Making up after a disagreement can be a very loving time. Having sex *where* you shouldn't makes for an exceptionally exciting time and although having sex with someone with *whom* you shouldn't is a wild and crazy adventure; it does not come without consequences.

You won't find anyone complaining about their sex lives during these circumstances. The problems occur when life is just sailing along on its normal course, in other words, in reality, where we spend most of our time. This is the time when couples have problems and complaints about their sex life.

As you've probably heard, men and women are as different as night and day when it comes to sexual needs and wants, which would explain why there are so many good books and manuals written about our sex lives. Women are much slower to heat up. We've heard them likened to a slow cooking oven, as opposed to men being more like microwaves. Instant heat. To a woman, making love has its beginnings in the morning when you have your first conversation. It's accumulative. If you've been snarky with each other all day, then expect to crawl into bed, roll over and have her anxious to make love to you, you're in for a disappointment. Men, on the other hand, seem to be ready and able at a moment's notice, regardless of what events took place an hour or ten minutes ago.

A woman thinks of sex as the icing on the cake. She admires and respects various aspects of her spouse and feels a love for him because of those attributes. Watching him play with the kids, cooking dinner or bringing her flowers, all play a part in the buildup to her wanting to make love to her husband. Making love to him is the icing on the cake. A man, using the same analogy, sees making love as *thee cake*. The physical act of making love plays a much bigger part for a man than the preceding emotional acts.

There is nothing average about making love. Sometimes everything falls together right and your sex life runs along smoothly with both partners happy and satisfied.

130

Other times, just like any other important part of your marriage, it's a rocky road and you need to talk about it. We found just talking to other people makes us realize that if we compare our lives to the magazines or movies, we are being unfair to our marriage. Movies and romance novels are great, but you are sabotaging yourselves by comparing your *real* relationship to that of a writer's fantasy. You'll lose every time. It would be great if our sex lives could be patterned after the romantic sex we see on the screen, but again, that is not reality. Every part of our marriage has its good days and bad days, and sex is no different. To give sex more power in the marriage than any of its other equal components is not giving a happy, healthy marriage its fair share.

Jeanine

I think part of the problem men and women have with sex is that it has different meanings for each gender. It has helped me to understand this better once Mark and I talked about our feelings on this issue. Mark once explained that when he initiates lovemaking and I tell him that I don't want to or don't feel like making love, he feels like I am saying "I don't love you", which is not what I am saying at all. Making love is only one of the many ways I feel we have of showing how much we love each other. To Mark, it is the major way of showing his love for me, so I can understand better why he is hurt (even though it comes out as anger) when I say I don't want to make love. Communicating about lovemaking helped to soothe our feelings. Mark understands that my love for him isn't any less just because I say "no" to his advances and I understand that this is his major way of showing me he loves me and need to make it clear that I don't love him any less when my desires don't match his. Once again, communication is the answer.

One of the best solutions we've heard of and seems to work for a lot of couples is "Date Night." Admittedly, it takes the spontaneity right out of your sex life, but the benefits often outweigh the loss of that one factor. The first step is agreeing on what is an acceptable frequency for sex for both of you. (No guys, *twice a day is not an option. On the other hand, once a month is not very reasonable either!) Once established, it must be agreed that those are the nights (or days) that will be for lovemaking. A nice dinner, some wine maybe, or anything that might make it a special night. I know it sounds pretty calculated, but once you try it, you will find a few things that are different in your relationship. For one, touching each other becomes a whole new wonderful thing. Before, when your partner touched you, gave you a hug, or a big kiss, admit it ladies, it was a "signal", right? If you responded to that hug, you were pretty much saying "let's hit the bedroom!". Now you can touch and be touched to your hearts desire and let it be the natural response that is so important in a relationship. You will also find, that as those Date Nights are approaching, you find yourself doing a little flirting and mentally planning some special surprises. It's not for everyone, but many couples have found it to be the perfect solution for them.*

Mark

I admit, I am one of those males that thinks there isn't enough sex in marriage. If it were up to me, we'd never get out of bed! But, I have learned over the years, that sex does not make the marriage. There have been times when our sex life was great, yet our marriage was falling apart in other areas, so my theory of "if only our sex life was better, we'd have a perfect marriage" went out the window. As we've grown older, I've seen that marriage is composed of many parts, each needing nurturing and attention. When one part of our marriage isn't going well, the rest of it seems to lose its steam also. We men seem to put so much focus on sex in the marriage and the importance of it, that we don't realize that it is just one part of the relationship, not the "be all, end all" to the union.

WORKSHEET

Describe your ideal date night

_____

_____

_____

_____

_____

_____

_____

Describe what you think your spouse's ideal date
night would be?

_____

_____

_____

_____

_____

What changes could be made to bring the two ideals
closer to the same experience?

_____

_____

Games People Play

GAMES PEOPLE PLAY

Relationships are not sporting events. Stop
wrestling for control. No one ever wins this kind of
match, except divorce lawyers.
Anonymous

Game playing in a marriage is one of the most wasteful efforts we know of. It is a waste of life's energy and the precious time we have together. There are many ways to play the game and we are all guilty of playing it in one way or another. Although there are several choices of games to be played in a marriage, they all end up with the same negative results.

Button pushing is probably one of the most common games we see. The effectiveness of this game is directly related to how long it has been played. If a spouse has been pushing a partner's particular button for many years and is still getting the same desired result, why would the game stop? These pointless games we play need two players and if we both continue to participate in the game, it will continue. For example, our friend is an immaculate housekeeper and takes great pride in her home and its cleanliness. When her husband wants to "get her goat" he will straighten up the magazines on the table or run his hand over a dusty spot and look at his hand with disgust. His insinuation that she is not a good housekeeper infuriates her to a degree you would not believe. We have seen the two of them play this game for years. It is the silliest thing we've ever seen. He gets hurt by something she says, and knows that attacking her housekeeping pride will hurt her and he pushes the button without even thinking. What is just as crazy is to watch her react the exact same way every time he pushes that button. It seems so obvious to us, on the outside looking in, that if she would not react, he would quit hitting the button. It would take a few times of having no reaction to his button pushing, or telling him to dust the table himself if it bothers him that much, but eventually that button wouldn't work the way it always has and he would quit pushing it. When pushing a button has no result, the button pushing stops.

Tug of war is another childhood game that we have brought along with us into our adult marriages. It is a game about "being right," which is very important to a lot of people. Most of the time, the issue just isn't worth the effort and even if it *is*, this is not an effective way to go about getting your point across. You will be amazed at the peace you feel inside to simply let go of the rope and walk away from the game! Much of the debating and arguing that goes along with this game is a matter of personal opinions or feelings you have about a situation in which there *are* no *right* answers. There are no right or wrong opinions or feelings, they just *are*. So you can play this game of Tug of War all day long and never gain an inch. This is a good time to ask, as Jerry Jampolsky does in *Love is the Answer*, "Do you want to be right or do you want peace?"

Do you remember, "sticks and stones may break my bones, but words will never hurt me?" Playground rap from the 50's. That little ditty had no truth to it when we were singing it way back then (because the words *did* hurt) and it doesn't ring true in our relationships today either. We can't tell you how many times we have had to apologize to each other for saying things we didn't mean during a heated discussion. When you run out of sensible words in a verbal battle, you start digging at the bottom of the barrel to keep your end going, saying anything that comes to mind. Those nasty little things we throw out there as desperate pieces of ammunition may make us feel like the conquering warrior at the time, but when the war is over and we're trying to heal the wounds, it's painful to see how you've hurt someone you truly love. You may have won the battle, but you have lost the war.

141

Twenty-one questions (or better known by some as "Guess why I'm angry") is a very common game played by all of us. We learned that game the first time we "pouted" and someone lovingly asked us, "What's the matter?" "Aha" we said, "manipulation works" and we've been using it ever since. All we need is someone willing to play the game with us. Clamming up and giving someone the "silent treatment" only adds fuel to the fire. To try and guess what is bothering someone is a real stab in the dark most of the time. I know we have gone for days without talking to each other (other than the essentials, like "pass the butter") and only one of us knows what the problem is. It's kind of silly when you think about it, but at the time, stubbornness overtakes sensibility and you think it's your "right" to be angry and if your spouse can't figure it out, then he or she must suffer your wrath until they do. It's laughable when you stand back and look at it, but in the heat of the moment it makes perfect sense.

Other than the common games we play, there are the ones we make up as we go along, customizing them for our own specific marriages. Even though these games are unique and effective for our particular situation, there is a similarity among all of the games we play. There are two basic rules to all the games: 1) It takes two people to play the game effectively and 2) Your consent is needed to play the game. Quitting the game is very simple. If you don't like the game, just let go of the rope and walk away from it. No one is winning.

Jeanine

I hate to admit how much time we have wasted playing all the games we've mentioned so far. (Didn't you wonder how we knew so much about all these games?) Seriously though, the sooner you begin to recognize the game playing that goes on in your marriage, the sooner you can put a stop to it. The games sometimes get to be such a habit with knee jerk responses that you play these games over and over without even realizing it and not knowing how to stop them. When you see how simple it is to stop the game by simply removing yourself as a player, you are starting to become a winner and bringing about some positive results. It also gives you your power back that you gave over to someone else when you entered the game. You give someone else the power to make you angry with a single word, a motion or some type of button pushing when agreeing to play games. By removing yourself from the game you not only regain your power and control but can begin to look at your relationship in a calm and sane manner rather than part of a game strategy.

Mark

We all have egos that are fragile, easily hurt and often get in the way of a good relationship. The ego in us puts itself first,

144

above anything and anyone else and whatever it needs to do to "win", it will do. Game playing is one of the ego's favorite challenges because egos are competitive and there is nothing like a good game of manipulation to challenge the ego. Being "right" sometimes takes the place of being understanding. The games we have played throughout the years have always created a "no win" situation. Eventually, one of the players gives up or concedes the game, but no one really won when you are walking away mad and hurt and misunderstood. We have all learned how to get what we want through game playing and we have all played the games at one time or another throughout our lives in our jobs and our relationships we have with others. Playing the same game with the same person year after year soon becomes a habit and we find ourselves playing the game without even realizing it. If you sit down and think about your relationship with your spouse, you will probably come up with several games that you have played over the years and will see the silliness of the game that you continue to play because in your mind, it works. On closer inspection, you may find that although you may win at the games most of the time, the end result doesn't put you anywhere near the finish line when it comes to satisfaction and success of your relationship.

WORKSHEET

What are some of our unproductive "games" we play

_____

_____

_____

_____

_____

_____

Names some button pushing that works every time for each of you?

_____

_____

_____

_____

_____

_____

Who is winning?

_____

Crossing The Line

DO NOT CROSS THIS LINE

CROSSING THE LINE

You have to decide what your highest priorities are
and have the courage, (pleasantly, smilingly, and
nonapologetically), to say "no" to other things.
And the way you do that is by having a bigger
"yes" burning inside. The enemy of the "best" is
often the "good."
Stephen Covey

We all have our own invisible lines that we have drawn as we've grown up, which separates what is acceptable to us and what is not. With two people making up a marriage, more often than not that line is in two different locations and the sooner we fully understand where those lines are, the better our marriage will be. Our morals, our acceptable and unacceptable behaviors, and the points where we become uncomfortable with a situation, are not always the same for each of us. What is acceptable to one spouse may be totally over the line for the partner. Sitting down and discussing these personal lines with each other is something that needs to be done if you expect your spouse to respect your boundaries. When you are married, you need to be aware of each other's standards to make it work. Do not make the assumption that everyone's boundaries are like yours. One would think that a lot of behaviors are obviously wrong to everyone. To assume this is to assume that we all think alike and we certainly don't do that. There are many "gray" areas when it comes to morals and what is "acceptable behavior". Are white lies, flirting with other people, or cheating on your taxes acceptable behavior? These are just a few issues that go either way for a lot of people. The big issues are more obvious to us, while the little ones have a way of chipping away at our marriages, so talk about those too. Just to look around in the world we live in, we see that everyone's idea of "good and evil" are not the same.

Forgiveness is a very large part of a successful marriage. Being able to forgive each other for mistakes made now and then is part of the continuing adjustment we make in our path together. Most things are forgivable, although some are harder than others to let go. And sometimes, we can forgive, but not so easily forget. Forgiving and the asking of forgiveness is a ribbon that runs throughout a good marriage.

There are times when forgiveness does not come easily, if at all, and those are the times when the "line" has been crossed. The destruction of many marriages comes with actions taken by one spouse or the other that are impossible to forgive and are definitely not forgotten. Once you cross the line, it is so much harder to get back to where you started. Crossing the line takes you beyond the "forgive and forget" area. We have seen so many marriages that could have been salvaged had they just not crossed the line, but once they crossed over they could not attain the forgiveness they needed to cross back. Even sadder is that most of these people found that the happiness and satisfaction they saw on the other side of the line, was not there when they got there. That old "greener grass" was actually an illusion.

There are many things that would be considered "crossing the line", but as we have said, that line is different for everyone. Two of our lines, for example, are infidelity and abuse. We can both be pretty certain that if either one of us crossed this line, our marriage would probably be over. There is always a chance we could work through it, if it were a "one time thing", but it would be quite a gamble to count on that. We've watched sadly as infidelity has broken up many of our friend's marriages. The infidelity line is one of the most difficult lines to return from. Once you have crossed that line, you are in a whole new arena, and even if you can find your way back, you've broken a trust that returns very slowly, if ever.

You can't put all the blame on your spouse for crossing a line they didn't know was there. For example, our friend's husband is a "hands on" kind of guy. Hands on his secretary, his female coworkers or any other woman that may be around. To him, it's all "in fun." He doesn't mean anything by it, and according to him, "It's not like I'm *sleeping* with them." His wife becomes angry at his behavior, assuming that because it has so obviously crossed her line of acceptable behavior, he would know how wrong he was in acting like this. *His* acceptable behavior line, however, wasn't crossed unless he *slept* with another woman. Little slaps and pats here and there were not considered "crossing the line" in his way of looking at things. So what may seem obvious to you does not make it obvious to anyone else and to be perfectly clear about it, you need to actually sit down and say, "This is not acceptable behavior to me and if it continues, we are going to have a problem."

Look for red flags or trends in certain areas of your marriage as you draw your lines. As mentioned earlier, family history will direct you to possible problem spots. Was your spouse hit often as a child? If so, draw that line now to save any trouble in the future by stating that hitting will not be acceptable in your house. Do you like the way your father-in-law treats your mother-in-law or your spouse? Pay attention, as it is likely that you will be treated in a similar manner. We learn from what we see, and even though we may not agree with how our parents raised us, or related to each other, that is what we had as an example and it will influence our child rearing and marriages in every way.

We all need to draw our imaginary lines in the dirt and let our partner know that they are asking for problems if they opt to cross it. The lines should be chosen with care and thoughtfulness and limited to a reasonable number, then, once you have stated your boundaries, stick to them. If you allow your spouse to cross one line, they will expect it to be okay to cross another, and little by little, your marriage *and* your line in the dirt will be unclear.

Marriage is hard enough maintaining the little things along the way. You will save yourselves so much grief and sorrow and most probably your marriage, if you will learn where the lines are and avoid crossing them at all costs. The little lines can trip up your marriage; the big lines can destroy it.

Jeanine

There is a security to me in having lines drawn and defined between Mark and I and also in knowing what Mark's lines are. I feel like I have some sort of unwritten agreement and knowledge that if these lines are not crossed, we can pretty much get through anything. I don't depend on this unwritten agreement as an insurance policy of holding us together, nothing is for sure in a marriage, but it is an important part of our relationship. I know that there is an understanding between us that if certain lines are crossed, we are opening ourselves up for some serious problems. Like Mark mentioned, there have been times in our 40 years that we have been tempted to cross the lines we have drawn for ourselves. It's hard to be going through a really rough time in a marriage while watching a few of your married friends "falling in lust", having a seemingly great time with some cutie pie from work. It makes you wonder why you are sticking with this dead marriage, being absolutely miserable, when there's this old flame calling and would love to show you how much he still cares. So you ask yourself, "Do I really want to exchange this cold, hateful, hurtful relationship with my spouse for some fun, romance and great sex? Do I really want to have an affair?" The answer is "YES!!! Give me some excitement and love. I need to feel good about myself!! Let's go for it!" Then the little woman on your other *shoulder says, "Lets think about this for a minute," and fortunately, for your marriage, you do. You realize that as great as this temporary affair might be (and you know it's going to be temporary because you've watched your friends go through it) it probably isn't worth throwing your marriage away. I know that this is not only one of Mark's lines, but mine too, so it would take maybe more than we had left to repair the damage done. Eventually, your marriage heals itself through some hard work and you are back in love* and *lust with the man you began your marriage with. I'm with Mark. I've never found anything or anyone worth crossing that line for and consequently risking our marriage.*

Mark

When we first got married, Jeanine made it very clear that there were only a couple of lines I ought not to cross. She basically let it be known that if I didn't hit her or have an affair, I got to live. Of course, she didn't actually say that but it was made very clear that these were two areas that she was very serious about. One of the things to look at is the family history of your spouse. Society has learned that tendencies to do things are evident in the past of our families. In both of our families, hitting was not an accepted way of communication. I was spanked as a child, but never out of

157

anger. It was always done when that seemed to be the appropriate punishment. No one was ever struck across the face or by hand. So hitting my wife has never really entered my mind. In some families, it is an accepted way of life, which makes you think twice about what we are teaching our children by example.

Having affairs, on the other hand, is a different matter. When my parents were married over 20 years, my father had several affairs. This led to the divorce of my parents after 28 years of marriage. Jeanine and I both learned from that experience of my parents that longevity in a marriage does not keep you "safe" from the temptations and pitfalls of life. As with all people, as we get older we look for validation of ourselves as human beings. We want to think we are still attractive to other people and have some worth to someone besides our spouse. This is especially true when we are going through difficult times. I confess, I have been guilty of looking around and thinking about affairs but I knew the price would be higher than I was willing to pay. My family is very sensitive to this, as all families probably are and I knew that part of the price of having an affair would be the possible loss of my children as well as Jeanine. Since I knew that this was a line Jeanine had definitely drawn, I have chosen not to cross it. It never seemed that worthwhile to me. My family has always been my priority, so knowing what lines I cannot cross and their consequences has kept me from a lot of trouble.

WORKSHEET

What are my lines that cannot be crossed?

_____

_____

_____

_____

What are my spouse's lines that cannot be crossed?

_____

_____

_____

_____

Have you made it clear to your partner where you line is? If not, why not?

_____

_____

_____

Do you think your partner's line is reasonable?

_____

_____

Forgiveness

FORGIVENESS

"Forgive, or Relive"
Anonymous

Every relationship in our lives, be it with friends, family or our children, reaches a place where forgiveness is called for. How we forgive, determines the future of that relationship. In a marriage relationship, however, it is not so easy to walk away from the situation or distance yourself when forgiveness is difficult or impossible.

We all make mistakes from time to time and need to be forgiven. It is tough to admit that we are not all perfect, but eventually, we all find ourselves in need of another's compassion in excusing our errors. Forgiving is part of the equation, while forgetting is equally important. Sometimes the forgiving is the easy part, while the letting go of the transgression is what is hard to honestly do.

Louise Hay, author of many great self-help books says, *"Forgiveness is a tricky and confusing concept for many people, but know that there's a difference between forgiveness and acceptance. Forgiving someone doesn't mean that you condone their behavior! The act of forgiveness takes place in your own mind. It really has nothing to do with the other person. The reality*

163

of true forgiveness lies in setting yourself free from the pain. It's simply an act of releasing yourself from the negative energy that you've chosen to hold on to."

So how do you forgive? The words can come out easily enough. The trick is meaning them. When we truly forgive someone, we need to honestly release the hurt, anger and fear of losing trust in our partner.

What we have learned over the last 40 years is that no one wins when we hold our forgiveness back. We may *think* we are winning by holding something over each other, but when we stand back and look at the situation, we are both miserable, and our stubbornness in not letting it go, is not accomplishing anything. While we are hanging on to the hurt and anger, it is eating us both up inside and affects everything about our relationship. We find it hard to move on to other, more important things in the growth of our marriage when one of us is hanging on to resentment over what the other has done. It is like we are looking through a screen of resentment at every part of our relationship and it isn't giving us a true picture. This festering anger comes up again and again when not forgiven. It may be dressed a little differently and not easily recognized as the resentment from the past, but if you peel away the layers, you will probably find that the anger you have is not about taking out the garbage or going over the budget.

Most of the circumstances that require forgiveness, like sharp words or other emotional hurts, can be undone or made up for with words and actions. Other more serious infractions such as crossing that line we've referred to, aren't so easily forgiven and much more difficult to forget. Understanding that we both are going to need forgiveness now and then keeps us open to exercising our flexibility. We find it to be emotionally exhausting to hang on to some incident for days when we have the choice of talking about it openly; voicing our concerns and then letting it go.

Often times, we think we are causing our partner the same suffering they have caused us by withholding our forgiveness, when in reality, we are hurting ourselves more than anyone. What we are actually doing is summed up by this quote: "Holding on to anger and resentment is like drinking poison and expecting someone else to die." As silly as that sounds, it is exactly what is happening when we keep churning the hurt and anger; reliving the incident over and over in our minds. It's a no win situation.

It may be obvious to you that you are in need of an apology, but not so obvious to your partner. As in all parts of a marriage, communication is the key. Don't keep each other guessing as to why you are hurt or upset. Talk about it.

Remember that forgiving someone is a compassionate act. It is not saying that what they have done is acceptable. It is not a green light for your partner to repeat the action. It is realizing that we are doing the best we can, and sometimes, we make mistakes. All of us. It is having the compassion and love to allow each other to be human.

Jeanine

Mark will tell you that I can hold a grudge longer than anyone he knows and I will admit that it is true. I have to say in my defense that I have gotten better at forgiving and forgetting over the years, but I still try to hang on now and then. My mother taught me a valued lesson once about forgiving.

Mark had a little too much to drink one night at a family gathering and decided to let my mom know how he really felt. It was not a happy family scene. He told my mother off while the rest of us sat there with our mouths open. Mark is usually very low key and it is not in his character to do something like this, but the rum showed us a new character. Needless to say, I was furious. The next morning, Mark was sick in more ways than one. He didn't even remember talking to my mom (did I say a lot of rum?) and I of course gave him an ugly detailed description of the scene. He felt terrible because he really did like my mom. He went over and talked to her and they ended up in a hug and all was forgiven. All was forgiven by my mother, mind you, but not by me. I held on to that incident for months, *I'm sorry to say, and could not forgive him for treating my mom that way. Even my* mother said *"Give it a rest, Jeanine....he had too much to drink and didn't mean it." But I hung on. And while I hung on, it ate at me whenever I would think about it. Eventually, I saw that no one was more sorry than Mark was and all the guilt in the world was not going to make him feel worse.*

Sometimes, it takes some major mistake on your part to realize that we need forgiveness. When you have been in the "need forgiving" area, it humbles you a bit and teaches you compassion.

Mark

All of us make mistakes. No one is perfect. We all need forgiveness at one time or another. If you are unwilling to forgive others, how can you expect others to forgive you?

There is another side effect of withholding your forgiveness. If you hang on to your anger at someone for a perceived or real transgression, that anger gets driven deep inside of you, first in your psyche, and eventually into your body, where it comes out as physical symptoms. In the book "Feelings Buried Alive Never Die", Karol Truman explains what has been shown to happen on a physical level when we bury feelings deep inside ourselves. There are many physical illnesses brought on by unresolved anger.

Jeanine and I finally figured out that it wasn't worth the wasted days of feeling bad, avoiding each other and hiding behind our walls of anger. All because we withheld our forgiveness.

WORKSHEET

Is there anything that you have not forgiven your spouse for?

_____

_____

_____

_____

Is there anything you have forgiven your spouse for, but are not able to let go of? What are the fears of letting it go?

_____

_____

_____

_____

_____

_____

Has there been a time when you needed forgiveness and received it? How did that make you feel?

_____

_____

Taking a Time Out

TAKING A TIME OUT

Friendship, like love, is destroyed by long absence,
though it may be increased by short intermissions.
                                                    Samuel Johnson

We used to have our kids take a "time out" when they were fighting with each other or having a fit over something. It gave them time to calm down, lose some steam and take a new look at the situation. Marriages need "time outs" now and then also, but unlike the kids, you need to recognize the need and call one for yourselves.

Our definition of "Time Out" is very broad. Time Out can be as simple as taking a half hour walk by yourself on the beach or as drastic as hopping on a plane and getting away for a month to think things over.

There are many times during our marriage that we have needed our own space and time away from each other. Sometimes, we recognized the need and made arrangements to get away from each other for a period of time and other times, one of us just left.

Having been through both types of separation, we can heartily suggest going to your separate corners cooperatively rather than storming out of the ring.

173

Many times we see the symptoms of our discontent cropping up in our marriages, but we wait until it is a full blown disease before we do anything about it. It is so much easier to mend a marriage one stitch at a time, than to try and patch up a gapping hole when there is little thread left on the spool. Taking small "time outs" as you go along will prevent the necessity of taking *"big* "time-outs" for marriages that have been hurting for a long time, and it's much easier on the heart.

Learn to become aware of the times when you are starting to nip at each other's heels for no apparent reason. Recognize and act upon the little irritations before they grow. Communicating, of course, is the easiest and probably most effective way to solve a problem, but sometimes talking just isn't enough or you just can't seem to talk to each other without starting a disagreement. This is a good time to go to your corners and do some thinking on your own. If possible, go to a friend's place for a weekend or to a parent's house for a week. Getting away from each other geographically gives you space you need and time to think, maybe write each other or talk on the phone.

There are several ways you can create your own space and each one serves a purpose. We realize it's not always easy to "get away" from your busy lives and tight

174

schedules. Your job, your children, and other responsibilities sometimes make it difficult, if not impossible, to remove yourself from your marriage for awhile, but we think it's important enough to make it possible. Sometimes a little inconvenience now can prevent a huge inconvenience and mistake in the future.

There are more serious separations that should be avoided at all costs, but are sometimes a last ditch effort when there seems to be no hope or relief in sight. We think there are a lot of couples who would be together today if they could have taken a time like this before rushing into a divorce or another relationship.

There have been a few times in our marriage when we have separated thinking that we were headed for divorce. It was a scary thing because we took a great risk of losing our marriage completely, and although that was not what we wanted, there seemed to be no alternative at the time. As much as we did not want to be divorced (on principle alone, say nothing about the effects on our children) we could not get along long enough to carry on a conversation with each other for more than a few minutes without an argument. There are times when you just can't get along no matter what and we all have had those times. Usually, those moments pass and we ask ourselves "What was *that* all about?" But when those times continue nonstop for months and into years, it's time to realize this is not going to work itself out on its own. Our choices were to continue with a marriage that was in constant turmoil and anger, or go our separate ways. So we went our separate ways. There was a sadness to the finality of our marriage and the history we had shared together. It felt like a death to us, an accidental death, not something we had planned on or meant to happen, but staying in the marriage at the time and working on it felt like we were beating a dead horse. This time we did not go away for a week to a friend's house, or temporarily move in with mom. We each got our own places, where we spent a lot of time reflecting on what was important to us, mourning our seemingly dead marriage, wondering what went wrong, how we could have fixed things and even looking at each other differently. There were qualities in each other we had forgotten about that we admired. We had let our negative, angry and even hateful feelings go on for so long without trying to fix anything that it took a month just to let go of those feelings. Only after we let go of the bad feelings could the good feelings come.

Absence not only "makes the heart grow fonder" but it gives the heart a chance to slow down and find its place again. Independently of each other, we realized what we had let go of and began to regret what had happened to our marriage. Luckily, neither of us had met anyone else to whom we turned to for love, romance and support, which is a risk we knew we took when we separated. We began again, as strangers. We found that when we were ready to communicate with each other, letter writing during these separations were our maps to getting back on the right track. We dated, talked for hours on the phone, wrote letters and renewed our appreciation for each other and what we had. We realized how fragile marriage can be and how it needs constant monitoring. Our marriage didn't fall apart in one day or over one argument. It fell layer upon layer without any support or intervention from us. What we realized were all the things we have been writing about in this book.

We do *not* suggest this kind of separation as a marriage-building tool. Our two major separations have turned out to be positive and enriching experiences for our marriage. We have learned and grown stronger from them and yes, they had very romantic endings. On the other hand, they were also hateful and hurtful times that could have been totally avoided with just a little effort put forth during our marriage when it was beginning to fall apart. We disrupted not only our lives, but many of the people around

177

us who love and care for us and most importantly, we risked losing each other as lifetime partners due to lack of attention to our marriage. Don't let your marriage get so far away from you that it takes such a major jolt to get it breathing again. It may kill the patient.

To us, a separation is the final step before a divorce, and we suggest it only as a last resort. Throwing away a marriage without giving it a last chance effort is not honoring the commitment you made to each other to begin with. It may not work out, and as you go your separate ways, at least you will know you tried everything you could. On the other hand, it may be just what you needed, and you may find yourself back on the right path, truly grateful that you took the time to try. You owe it to yourself, each other and your marriage to try everything you can before announcing the marriage has ended.

Jeanine

I have talked to so many women at the end of their relationships that have said "There is no way in hell that I could ever love that man again." I have to laugh (to myself, of course) because I have been there and like these women, would have bet my life savings that I would never be able to rekindle feelings for Mark. The good news is that many of these women are back with their husbands and "in love" again. We all assume that once you "fall out of love" or even worse, begin to hate the person you are married to, there is no turning back. We look at that person and think we could never care for, respect or make love to them again, because there is so much anger, resentment and disgust that to imagine this in our wildest dreams is not a possibility. I think it's heartening to know that this is not true. You can fall in and out of romantic love with your spouse over and over. I remember going beyond the anger to the point of not even caring, which in my mind seems worse. With the anger, at least you have some feelings for each other, where not having any feelings for each other seems hopeless. During our separation, my sister asked "Aren't you afraid that Mark will find someone else?" and at the time I truly wanted him to find someone else because I felt bad for him being alone. Strange feelings, but it shows that even as much as we were "out of love" with each other at the time, it was possible to find our way back to being crazy in love again. So please trust me in knowing that no matter what your feelings are or are not for your spouse, they can and will change if only given the chance.

Mark

Isn't love grand? Once we get married we think it is just like the movies, we live happily ever after. We wake in the morning, kiss each other and begin another day of just being together. Well, I can tell you it doesn't work that way. I know the Hollywood types say that for the magazines, but have you ever noticed they keep saying it every two or three years about their new love?

Sometimes we need to be apart. Sometimes we are just tired of each other and really don't like being together. Jeanine has been known to go to Alaska where she has family to "visit". Well, I am here to tell you, in the early days when she did that, chances are we weren't getting along all that well and we just needed some time alone. That has always worked for us. The old cliché "absence makes the heart grow fonder" is really true. (Today, I'm happy to say, her Alaska trips are more about visiting her family than about needing a break from our marriage.)

These visits have been a part of our time out system. We just agree to be apart while we think things through. Now this

180

will not work for everyone for a variety of reasons. Work gets in the way, kids are being raised, and the list goes on. We are lucky at this stage of our lives. The kids are raised and Jeanine works out of the house. All I know is that this form of time out has saved our relationship several times. If one of you cannot get away for an extended period of several weeks, at least do it for a week or even a weekend.

A word of caution: This is not a time to sow wild oats or rekindle old relationships. That would be the quickest way to disaster. It is a time to reflect and analyze your feelings. To see what it would be like to be alone, without your partner. To maybe do some things that you have given up for you spouse. I am talking about the little things that aggravate you, not the major areas that would cause a complete failure of the relationship. Most of the time you will find that those little things that you have given up, the ones that only come to mind when you aren't getting along, aren't really that important to you now.

WORKSHEET

If you needed to be away from each other to sort things out, where would you go?

_____

_____

_____

_____

_____

_____

_____

What are some things you would do with your time apart from each other?

_____

_____

_____

_____

_____

_____

Grow Old Along With Me

THE BEST IS YET TO BE

Grow old along with me! The best is yet to be.....
Robert Browning

Whether you have been married a few years, 25 years or in the planning stages of your wedding, know that there is a future filled with rewards from the work you are putting into your relationship now. The "gold watch" or the "bonus" from years of marriage cannot be seen or worn or spent, but felt by an invisible connection between you and your partner. Sharing your house, your bed and your children is the surface part of a good marriage, sharing your thoughts and spirits are the best part. Knowing you will be with each other after the kids are raised, your friends have moved away and your parents have died, is a comfort like no other we know of.

It is a good feeling to know that your partner will be with you through the best and the worst parts of your life. Here is a friend who is offering unconditional love, appreciating you for who you are and for who you have become. To be able to sit in a room with another person, not saying a word, and not feeling like you should be talking, yet knowing there is an invisible bond between you, is like the safety you feel when coming home. To share common thoughts and feelings with someone over a period of 40 years is a history no one can take away. To exchange looks with someone and know what they are thinking, and better yet, know you are thinking the same thing, is a bond shared by few. It is something you don't share with anyone else.

Being away from each other for a while makes us realize how much a part of each other's lives we have become. There is a part of us that is missing when we are not close with each other. We are still whole people by ourselves, but we are enhanced when we are a part of each other's lives.

These feelings and bonds do not happen overnight. Like anything worth having, it takes time, work and patience. There are days when things aren't going so smoothly that it doesn't seem worth the effort. More often, there are days when you look at your partner and understand completely why you are working to make your marriage stronger everyday. There is joy in the journey as well as heartache. The goal of a good marriage is to create a path where the joys far outnumber the struggles. As we look at our marriage, we know that everything we have done has been worth the energy we have put into it. That alone, gives us the love, the strength and the desire to keep on building. Although 40 years seems like a long time to us, we feel like newlyweds when compared to others who have been together 60 years. We still have many challenges and changes ahead of us. We never take for granted that our years behind us will support the years ahead of us. We can't stop caring, grooming and appreciating our marriage simply because it has worked this long. The tools we have shared with you are the same ones we continue use in our marriage on a daily basis. We sharpen our tools regularly, we add new ones now and then and we pull out some old standbys that haven't seen the light of day in years when we need them. We never assume that because we are walking on air today, that tomorrow or next month are going to naturally follow suit. Not unlike a garden, our marriage is tended to, nourished and appreciated.

Jeanine

I sat in my office one day and watched an old couple as they walked along the street. You couldn't tell which one was holding the other up, but you knew that they had been supporting each other for many years. It made me think about our lives together as a couple. It is hard to imagine us at that stage of life, but it's inevitable. I asked myself if we would be holding each other up when that day came? Can I count on Mark to keep me from falling and breaking my hip? Can he count on me to visit him at the nursing home every day for months and months if need be? That is one, and only one, of the rewards of having a lifetime partner. Today, we live our lives in the fast lane (or at least we are on the freeway still) and don't give much thought to that time in our future, but it will come. It gives me peace to know that my partner is going to go there with me. We are, more than likely, going to face our "senior years" together. We will take on that challenge much like we did our first year of marriage, our kids going through their teen years, our mid-life crisis' and everything in-between. We'll do it together, taking turns being the leader, holding each other up, but most importantly, as a loving team. That thought makes me smile.

Mark

Perhaps the best part of marriage is the growing old together. Although I don't consider Jeanine and I old (except in dog years) we have over 40 years together. Everything in our life together is better. We understand each other pretty well by now. We know when to give the other person a wide berth, when they need sympathy, and even when we just need a hug. We raised our kids, our careers are stable, and we have a little more money to do the things we want to do. The thought of not being together has not been entertained in a long time. As you have read, we have been close to losing each other, even separated twice, but I never thought we wouldn't be together in our later years.

We have a bond. A love that is forever. We both believe we are supposed to be a couple, and that somehow the Universe meant for us to live this life together. For that I am grateful.

As a couple, you need a vision that includes thoughts of growing old together. Make it part of your plan.

Jeanine was talking about coloring her hair because she was getting a few gray hairs. I'm against it. I love those gray hairs. They represent our life in my mind. I see our past in those little gray hairs. They are a reminder of how much we have been through, and how our love has always won out. The gray tells me we've been together a long time and I look forward to seeing more of them. I can only hope that Jeanine feels the same about my emerging bald spot.

WORKSHEET

Describe you marriage, in detail, twenty years from now.

_____

_____

_____

_____

_____

_____

_____

_____

_____

_____

_____

_____

_____

_____

_____

_____

_____

Thank you for reading our book. We hope we have contributed in some way to help you develop a stronger, more loving and long lasting relationship.

Jeanine & Mark

Please visit our website:
Marriageworksthebook.com

Made in the USA
Charleston, SC
10 January 2011